THE PEPPER TREE KINGDOM

Azalea Art Press
Southern Pines, North Carolina

ISBN: 978-0-9899961-2-9

Dedication

꙳꙳꙳꙳꙳

This memoir is in honor of my precious
wife of almost fifty years, Mahin; her sister
Esmat; my two beloved daughters, Ladan
and Rana; my son-in-law, Sam Brabo;
and my five grandchildren: Dominic, Isaac,
Addison, Grace and Eli.

And to my many American and Iranian
friends who have supported and helped me
navigate the sometimes rough waters
of my life journey.

Author's Note

>>>)) ((((«

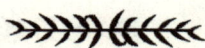

This is a work of nonfiction. The facts in
this story are true insofar as my memory serves;
however, certain names have been changed
and, in some cases, events have been condensed.

CONTENTS

>>>>>)((((<<

Preface

>>>)) ((<<<

For many years, I hesitated to write about any dimension of my life. I never wanted to prepare and distribute an autobiography. Such an effort seemed egotistical and self-serving. And, after all, who would be interested in reading about the details of my life except my own family? I was never sure about the level of interest even my family members might have in learning about me.

With the emergence of the literary genre of the memoir, however, I began to think differently. A memoir has many of the characteristics of an autobiography but focuses on a particular part or dimension of a person's life rather than the details of his/her entire life. It is, in Gore Vidal's words, "how one remembers one's own life" or a particular dimension of it. This made more sense to me. I could focus on a legacy narrative about a life passion without including what I considered to be unimportant details.

The humorist Will Rogers once said something wise about including the good things and omitting the bad things, but contrary to that advice I decided at the outset to tell all. Otherwise, I don't believe I would have benefitted as much from the effort as I did. This volume has provided the opportunity to reflect over the many years of searching for my identity and has proved to be quite therapeutic.

The reader may find some of the incidents and situations in this volume to be amusing. Some chapters reveal my naiveté and lack of social skill, but no attempt has been made to separate my private from my public life. Altogether, I hope my story clearly outlines the intensity of my search for an identity—from childhood to the present.

Franklin T. Burroughs
November 2013

Chapter 1

To Run No More:
My Escape from Islamic Iran

I didn't escape because I wanted to. I had to. Slipping from my beloved haven that was rapidly becoming an inferno represented the only alternative to a life plagued with uncertainty. I had to accept that neither my family nor I would be shown any mercy nor would I be permitted to live what I considered a halfway normal life in the Islamic Republic. I could not entertain the only probable alternative to flight—imprisonment.

During the drive from my place of hiding to the airport, the atmosphere in the car was tense. No one uttered a sound except my wife, Mahin, and me. We made every attempt to relieve the obvious tension by bantering about our likely return to Iran in the near future, what I planned to do in the U.S. and how I had enjoyed Iran and the family.

"Do you think they will actually let you leave?" Mahin whispered in English.

"I don't see why they wouldn't," I responded. "I have done nothing wrong."

"I hope you'll be able to find a job in the U.S.," she said, slightly breathless.

"Why shouldn't I be able to with my experience? The U.S. Government and corporations are always looking for people with experience like mine," I said.

"Will the children be able to adjust to life in the U.S.?" Mahin wondered.

"Why shouldn't they? They're young and adaptable," I responded.

Sadness filled me throughout the ride. I felt I would probably never again see my brother-in-law who was driving the car. I might not ever be able to attend another family gathering. But I tried to put on a smiley face. Mahin did her best to encourage me by confirming over and over that she was sure that things would work out for the best.

As soon as we arrived at the airport, I said goodbye to my brother-in-law and kissed Mahin. I almost felt like Judas kissing Jesus in the garden. I wondered if authorities would seize her for allegedly being an accomplice of an American spy or for simply being the wife of an American under suspicion of opposing the Islamic regime. The kiss was short. I reluctantly left Mahin at the door of the airport waiting room.

Most often, I would dress as fashionably as possible while living in Iran, but the day I went to Mehrabad International Airport for the last time, I was dressed in very casual clothing. I had on a nondescript pair of dress slacks, a simple sport shirt and a well-worn pair of loafers. Under no circumstances did I want to draw attention to myself.

I approached the check-in counter with considerable fear and trepidation. Dressed in regular street clothing, the passenger-service agent seemed to be glowering at me, and I imagined him saying, "Welcome to Imam Khomeini International Airport. I will check you in and from here you will be transported to Evin." Evin was the notorious prison where many prisoners were jailed and tortured.

Without making direct eye contact with the agent, I checked in one small suitcase, the only piece of luggage I was allowed to take with me. That case contained a silk rug, one pair of pants and a few personal items. The carpet dominated the space. I declared the rug a prayer carpet, thereby facilitating its export without excessive questioning. At that time, only carpets used for worship could be exported.

Throughout the check-in process, I only carried a small briefcase and a two-carat diamond embedded in a wad of chewing gum in my mouth. The gum prevented the customs authorities from detecting the stone. The sophisticated security systems commonly used in airports today were not yet in operation in Tehran at the time.

Both the carpet and the diamond were intended to serve as financial backups in case of an emergency in the U.S. I was uncertain about finding employment in the U.S., at least for a time, even though Mahin and

I had feigned job assurance during the ride to the airport. I had been away for fifteen years and many of my contacts had retired or passed on. Perhaps the carpet and/or the diamond could be sold for cash.

I waited silently while the attendant weighed and checked the bag, my heart skipping beats and my brain flooded with suspicion and questions. What if the attendant did beckon authorities to arrest me? Did the attendant have my U.S. passport? Would he give it to me with stamped permission to leave the country? The Government of the Islamic Republic had possessed my passport for more than a week and could have forbidden me to leave or even arrested me at the check-in counter. Was my name on the forbidden-to-leave list?

Slowly, the attendant shuffled the papers in front of him. He didn't say a word but merely continued to stare at me. I avoided his gaze but felt the knot in my stomach growing larger. Finally, he picked up what I knew was my passport, stamped it and handed it to me without a word. I almost screamed, "Free at last!"

While boarding the Swiss Airline jet that November morning in 1979, I began to feel like an escape artist. I had not performed a magic disappearing act, nor had I been put in a container like the Virginia slave known as Henry "Box" Brown who had himself stored in a relatively small box and shipped to an abolitionist destination in 1849. I had, however, managed to elude the Islamic Republic authorities long enough to be granted permission to leave the country. I scaled the proverbial wall during the gap between the issuance of my clearance to leave the country and the entry of my name on the list of those individuals forbidden to depart.

As I approached the gate where the shuttle waited to take me to the plane, I suddenly felt compelled to stop and look back into the airport terminal. Thousands of memories flooded my mind: my grand arrival in Tehran, my experiences while living in the city, my travels throughout the Middle East and now my forced departure. Even my development as a person and my pre-Iranian days filled my mind. I stood only a minute and then practically ran through the gate to the shuttle.

Once in the air, I ordered a double Scotch and removed the diamond from my mouth, fearful that I might inadvertently swallow it in an emotional moment. The stewardess quietly responded that she would arrange a drink for me once the plane had exited Iranian air space. She kept her word, and, boy, did I enjoy that Scotch.

Even before I had a sip of my drink, however, I succumbed to uncontrollable sobs for more than two hours. I hadn't realized under how much pressure I had been functioning during the takeover of the U.S. Embassy and my ten days in seclusion until I was able to relax and not fear for my life.

I left Iran under uncertain circumstances but with reliable transportation under the supervision of trustworthy professionals. I wasn't a victim—perhaps a potential victim—attempting to escape the rising persecution of Islamic fundamentalism. I was, however, attempting to escape dangers and preparing for my wife, Mahin, and daughters Ladan and Rana to join me at the earliest possible date.

I did not take a covert route out of Iran. No government facilitated my departure. No organization sponsored my flight first to Switzerland and then on to the U.S. I left behind some fifteen enjoyable years of my life and returned to the country of my birth and citizenship, a country that I had never been able really to call home or fully relate to.

Mahin and I had begun to lead an existence of fear and uncertainty under the Islamic Republic. The U.S. Embassy had been seized and many of its staff members incarcerated in the embassy compound. Our daughters could not continue to enjoy the privileges and freedom they had once had. As a family, we began to fear unwarranted government retribution because of my U.S. citizenship and ties.

I reluctantly fled Iran into self-imposed exile; my flight meant I would be permanently away from the place I fondly called home. Shortly after my departure, my name was placed on a list of people not allowed to leave the country. Only in recent years has my name been removed from the list, possibly allowing a safe visit to Islamic Iran. But, to this day, I remain fearful of what might happen if I chose to visit the country again.

My self-imposed exile did not represent a protest against persecution; it reflected only a fear of possible persecution. I was not attempting to isolate myself in an effort to devote time to a particular project except to find a new life with my family.

My departure from Iran meant an escape from a possible Benjamin-Button syndrome in which aspects of premature aging manifest early in life. I hoped the departure would permit a relatively normal aging process.

The journey from Iran to Switzerland remained peaceful. Imbibing whiskeys quieted my nerves and subordinated any worries about the future or rejoicing about escaping the Islamic Revolution untouched physically. In Switzerland and the flight from there to the United States offered time to become agitated and worried. Not even whiskey could help.

I hesitate to declare that my destiny was predetermined by an irresistible power, but unusual circumstances have resulted in an unusual life for me. My natural order in the cosmos has not only been invigorating, but totally unexplainable, at times frightening, but very inspiring. Life, for sure, has never been dull.

Chapter 2

>>>>)) ((<<<<

The Psychological Hitchhiker

Who am I? Am I who I think I am? Am I too often a hypocrite? Am I weak, or am I strong? These questions have challenged me much of my life.

In The *Book of Love: Poems of Ecstasy and Longing*, the Persian poet, Rumi, asks the question "Who am I?" In considering who he might have been, Rumi was probably not concerned as much about his future as he was about his past identity and the influence that identity had on the present. Like many Persians, he reached back, not forward, in developing an identity for himself. Rumi also wrote this: "Lo, for I to myself am unknown, now in God's name what must I do?"

For most of my life, I have asked myself the question that Rumi posed: "Who am I?" As a child, I constantly struggled with my identity and frequently tried to find my real self. I generally played alone and often assumed dual, even multiple, roles during my playtime. I was simultaneously a teacher and a student. I would administer and accept discipline in the classroom or on the playground.

Rumi's longing to know who he was resonated with me from the time I first heard about his ruminations. His father was a theologian and mystic; my father a country preacher and mystical hardliner. Rumi's questions helped me accept spirituality without the legalism and motivated me to ask this question consistently: "Can I find out something about my identity through discovering the self?"

In an article that appeared in "Christianity and Crisis," March 24, 1946, Dietrich Bonheoffer asked whether he was what other people said he was, or was he primarily what he knew about himself? He questioned whether he was one person or the other, or was he both persons—a split personality. In the latter part of his essay, Bonheoffer worded his quandary in this way:

"Who am I? This or the other?
Am I one person today and tomorrow another?
Am I both at once? A hypocrite before others,
And before myself a contemptibly woebegone
weakling?"

In the Book of 2 Samuel, Chapter 7, Verse 18 in the Bible, King David sat before the Lord and asked the question: "Who am I, O Sovereign Lord and what is my family, that you have brought me this far?" King Solomon, one of the wisest men to ever live, seemed occupied with the same question.

The Hindu philosopher Ramana Maharshi posed the same identity question that King David had asked centuries before in his book entitled *Who am I?* In the volume about self-enquiry, Maharshi suggests that only after one knows who he/she is can he/she attain happiness and the highest level of love.

Sufism poses the question of who we are or who we have been. Related questions broached in Sufi teachings include: "Where did I come from, and where will I go?"

While the related Sufi questions began to concern me only after several years of searching, the questions about who I was occupied my mind from early childhood. In my interactions with others, I often detected in my own behavior actions or statements that could have been interpreted as being inconsistent, but my continuing search for my "true self" remained consistent. That search and what I discovered about myself made me one person today and another tomorrow. I preferred what was often viewed as inconsistency to a designation of a "contemptibly woebegone weakling."

Assuming dual roles resulted in a tendency to take on a persona or personae I thought another individual or group expected me to have. My purpose in the apparent duplicity was not to be devious but to please and to try and figure out where I stood on a particular issue and who I was in relation to the individual or group. I didn't necessarily have a specific opinion or conviction since I hadn't been brought up to challenge ideas or authority openly.

Throughout my school years, I usually kept to myself. I had few friends and in secondary school, chose to major in Latin, which attracted only two or three other individuals. I could never compete in athletics. I simply didn't have the strength or the aptitude. Every year I signed up and participated in "corrective gym."

In college, I dabbled in intramural politics and enjoyed the financial security of a four-year, full-tuition scholarship and frequent grants from the California Parent-Teacher Association. During my senior year, I served as mediator between the outgoing and incoming college administrations. The mediation was conducted quietly without the knowledge of most of the students under the rubric of the student organization then known as the Academic Life Committee, of which I was the president. The mediator role required me to be as objective and discreet as possible and kept me from developing lasting ties with any one individual on either administrative side or even fellow students.

Toward the end of my senior year, I met a beautiful young Persian lady named Mahin and immediately fell in love. It didn't take long for me to ask Mahin to marry me. She agreed to the marriage after I promised not to make music my career and we were married in January 1959. We both continued our studies until 1964, when Mahin completed her Master of Science degree in Public Health, and I was awarded my Doctor of Education degree in Middle East Studies and Comparative Education.

As I reminisce about the early years with Mahin, I realize I still felt insecure but attempted to be who I thought she wanted me to be. She encouraged me to be a person who could accept himself and not worry about what others thought of him. She married me for who I was and promised to be, not for what others thought about me. She saw in me something I couldn't see in myself at the time of our marriage. She felt I could succeed in any field I chose while I still harbored doubts about my capabilities. She possessed a keen and open mind, and her openness encouraged me to intensify my search for an identity and my academic pursuits.

Mahin's support and belief in me were evident in the way she checked in with me often about how I felt.

"What do you really want to be, a professor or lawyer?" she would inquire.

My answer would often be, "I am not certain. Do you think I am capable of becoming an attorney?"

"Certainly you are," she would answer. "Now that you have agreed to forget about a music career, a career my family would have had difficulty accepting, what do you really want to be? What is it that really inspires you?"

Finally, I admitted to both Mahin and myself that the Middle East, particularly Iran, was my passion and had been for many years.

Mahin and I left Los Angeles for Iran shortly after graduation in 1964, took up residence and remained there for more than fourteen years. Our two daughters, Ladan and Rana, were both born in Tehran. I felt very comfortable in Iran and loved the culture as well as Mahin's family and the many friendships I developed. For the first time in my life, I began the journey toward discovering my true self.

The Islamic Revolution forced our return to the United States with few possessions. Upon returning, we worked hard to eke out a living, doing almost anything that came our way. I served as a marketer and developer. Mahin had her own small business and later performed several functions in local banks. Our financial setback and return to the United States seemed to bury or at least hide my sense of identity that had been unfolding in Iran.

Years later, we finally arrived at a point where Mahin said, "I don't think either one of us has to work any longer. Let's enjoy ourselves." We both thought we could take life a little easier, and it was at that point that sadly and unexpectedly, Mahin passed on. I was left to cope without my close companion of fifty years—my sense of "self" challenged yet again.

Mahin has been gone several years now, and while I still miss her and will do so as long as I live, I feel her longtime support has finally allowed me to feel comfortable in my search for an identity. Mel Schwartz, a psychotherapist and marriage counselor, suggested that people posing the question "Who am I?" are often struggling with their identity and are attempting to find "a core sense of themselves." Whatever the impetus might be, the discovery of who we are is an ongoing process and represents a desire to attain an increasingly deeper sense of self. That said, I accept and thrive on the challenge of finding my ultimate self. I have come to enjoy the role of the "psychological hitchhiker."

Chapter 3

>>>>)) ((((<<

The Pepper Tree Kingdom

Most imaginative kingdoms are inhabited by a unique collection of magical creatures, but no such creatures have graced my Pepper Tree Kingdom. I have, from the outset, been the main kingdom dweller, and either the actual tree or its graceful image has served to protect me during both good times and periods of depression and psychological uncertainty.

The California pepper tree became a major player in my psyche early in my childhood in Wilmington, California. Wilmington, a small, somewhat depressed town in the Los Angeles Harbor, boasted few places of beauty or natural plants of interest. Most of the plants were either refineries or canning facilities. The blooming wisteria vines located in the city park prompted an annual celebration of several days, but I do not recall any other plant or tree even encouraging a lethargic response. The excitement over nature seemed limited to the lovely wisteria blossoms.

The pepper tree that graced the vacant lot next to the cottage where my paternal grandmother, Grandma Dickson, lived, however, represented the best of nature to me. The tree was not a member of an urban forest but did add greenness to what otherwise was a dismal setting. It boasted drooping branches and bright green leaves. Its small, white summer flowers gave way each year to rose-colored berries in the fall that were about the size of black pepper corns. It reminded me of a weeping willow tree with great strength and resistance.

One branch of the tree housed my "rope throne" and permitted a view of the street, the local hotel and the small two-room shanties in which Grandma Dickson lived. That branch allowed me to swing back and forth and protected me from the gaze of passersby. I was partially hidden even from the pedestrians who used the vacant lot on which the tree was located as a shortcut to the downtown area.

I didn't mind the pedestrians passing through "my territory" as long as they didn't linger or attempt to disturb my peace and quiet through extended conversation. I viewed myself as "King of the Pepper Tree Kingdom" and the only citizen of the kingdom. The pedestrians were sojourners in a foreign land that they simply did not understand; I didn't have the patience or ability to explain my kingdom to them.

When the pepper tree first cast its spell on me, I was completely unaware of its Peruvian origin or its mystical influence on philosophers like Jiddu Krishnamurti. Its legend and lore quickly spoke to me of ancient cultures and spiritual insight. The pepper tree symbolized a certain brand of freedom and individuality, enhanced and broadened my view of eternity and pointed to a path promising to lead to wisdom and compassion. It awakened an inquisitive spirit in me, a determination to experience an insightful way of living.

Through the years, the memory of the pepper tree has encouraged me to make every effort to adopt a nuanced spiritual position and look at ideas from a variety of perspectives and in greater depth. The memory has inspired me to seek the truth, which casts no shadow and tolerates no gloom. It has helped me engage in the sacred realm while avoiding fanaticism.

I failed to gather literal seeds from the pepper tree in Wilmington, but I have fortunately enjoyed the fruits of the figurative seeds planted in my psyche. The pepper tree has, along with my precious wife of forty-eight years, served as the inspiration and basis for my continuously evolving, imaginative kingdom.

Chapter 4

>>>>))(((<<<

Wilmington's Social Contrast

A recent trip to South Africa awakened childhood memories of the run-down condition of the cottages bordering my Pepper Tree Kingdom. Granted,
the cottages could not technically be designated a *favela*
or shanty town. They were not improvised dwellings
built of plywood, corrugated metal or sheets of plastic,
nor were they on the periphery of a city. They boasted
electricity, sewage, numbered streets and at least some
sanitation. They were in the center of the drab town of
Wilmington, California, near the main fire station.
Some of the residents probably even had telephones.

The cottages, however, constituted a mid-town
slum. Their construction was substandard. An adjacent
building had begun to fall apart from a lack of upkeep
and maintenance. Only the few stucco apartments
fronting the lot on which the cottages sat were passa-
bly clean. In reality, the cottages were shacks that
housed impoverished people, whom society for the
most part had left behind. They comprised a squatter
settlement where the renters were experiencing down-
ward mobility and the germination of feelings of des-
peration and despondency.

Two of the renters were a married couple, both of whom were alcoholics. They must have been in their late sixties but looked much older. The husband worked during the day and arrived home around 4:30 to 5:00 p.m. As soon as he arrived, both he and the wife would begin drinking, and it wouldn't be long before they would begin to fight. They would curse each other and scream at the tops of their voices.

"Why were you late today?" the wife would yell.

"I had some work I had to finish before I could leave," the husband would answer.

"I don't believe you," the wife would call out. "Are you sure you weren't out drinking with your friends when you should have been home with me?"

This type of dialogue would continue for at least two hours each afternoon, and the screaming could be heard for at least two blocks. But no one dared to complain. The couple would have been on the complainers' case immediately and would have made it difficult for them to maintain their residency in the shanties. Money was very scarce and a roof over one's head took preference to an hour or two of cursing and drunken carrying on.

I had to share the bathroom with the two lushes when I spent the night with Grandma Dickson, and I would never know when one of them would try to break the bathroom door down while I was relieving myself. The one wanting to use the facility would bang on the door and yell, "How long are you going to take in there? I need to use the bathroom."

If I answered, "I will be finished soon," the attempted intruder would say in a loud voice, "Why do you take so long? You have had all day to relieve yourself. It's my turn to use the bathroom."

Whichever one wanted in would shake the door knob and shout, "You better hurry, or I'll have to break the door down."

Whether that was a true statement or not, I never knew, but I did hurry, sometimes almost to my own detriment.

Both the husband and wife terrified me even though they were probably harmless, but they didn't seem harmless, and when they would get very loud or would attempt to force their way into the bathroom while I was the occupant, I would cut my use of the facility short and fly to my Pepper Tree Kingdom during the day and wherever I could hide at night.

One family of renters consisted of a father, mother and a grown daughter. The mother was partially blind, and the daughter suffered from a debilitating skin disease. They wore ragged, outdated clothing and made every effort to avoid interaction with other individuals.

A third group of renters included a frail grandfather, a self-designated, high-school debutante and a snuff-dipping mom. The grandfather got tired of struggling for his existence while the high-school daughter longed for prestige her family's position in society denied her. The snuff-dipper could eject saliva forcibly from her mouth into her poor-man's spittoon with the accuracy of a rifle and the velocity of a north wind.

The husband-and-wife managers of the cottages occupied a two-bedroom house adjacent to my Pepper Tree Kingdom. The wife kept herself busy registering voters. When I was visiting with my grandmother, the husband would invite me to watch wrestling on television with him. He enjoyed talking with me, and I enjoyed hobnobbing with the major players in our small world.

"Would you like to watch the wrestling matches with me tonight?" he would ask. "Mrs. Johnson is busy registering people for the upcoming elections."

"I would like that," I would answer. "Who is wrestling?"

"I have no idea," he would answer. "But whoever it is will put on a good show." Incidentally, the television had a screen so small that only with a bubble could the observer decipher the picture.

The dilapidated building adjacent to the shanty-like cottages housed a strange shoe cobbler's shop and a brother and sister who could hardly speak English. Few people entered the shop, and those who did likened the interior of the building to a Halloween horror studio. Once a year, the cobbler loaded the steps of the building with women's pointed shoes from the early 1900s, which made the building look even more menacing.

About a block from the shanty town and horror studio was the only hotel in the small town. Situated on the main street, the brick building struck my young, imaginative vision as beautiful and upscale, but the daughter of the hotel manager seemed to me even more sophisticated and privileged. She and her family had quarters on the fourth or fifth floor of the building and attendants to clean their apartment, prepare their food and care for their needs. I imagine the services provided by the attendants were not as extensive as I thought, but I would often sit on my rope throne and look longingly at the quarters and attempt to picture the privileged life the daughter and her parents enjoyed. I envied their lifestyle.

"Do you enjoy living in a hotel?" I would ask the daughter when I saw her at school.

"It's okay," she would answer. "After all, Dad has to make a living."

I always thought her response showed a lack of respect for me. I longed for an invitation to see their quarters in the hotel and perhaps share some cookies with her. I never was able to talk my way into the quarters that intrigued me so much.

The contradictions between the derelict shanty town comprised of the cottages and the cobbler's shop and the hotel one block away created a strange picture of urban life. The contrast could have served as a template for redevelopment. It certainly emphasized the differences between the poor and the somewhat more privileged. I knew I was among the poor and hated every minute of my existence, even in the early stages of my childhood. I was about five years of age at the time. I often fretted over the fact that I had to share a bathroom with two drunkards while the hotel manager and his family had private quarters and maid service. Since I didn't have a bed, I slept on the floor while my grandmother occupied a bed that she had to roll into her closet each morning so that a makeshift sofa could be available. If my Dad's brother, Uncle Otis, came to visit, he was often inebriated and would sleep in the kitchen, keeping me from even getting a glass of water at night. Even the green color of the outside walls of the shacks depressed me.

The contrast between the "haves" and the "have-nots" never let me forget the differences in social class and my particular position as well as that of my family in society. I tended to label myself by my heritage and fret over my predetermined membership in the "lower class." The contrast also reinforced in me the American dream of completing my education and improving myself. It encouraged me to strive toward "who I could become." The physicians and particularly the dentist for whom Grandma Dickson cleaned offices inspired me to work hard and dream big.

Chapter 5

Venturing From the Kingdom:
A Grandmother-Grandson Relationship

The first time she set eyes on me, I could have
been naked, having just been born. Perhaps she didn't
see me until sometime later when I innocently looked
at the world with fresh eyes, a smile here, and a cry
there. Perhaps she didn't see me until I was an older
child. I don't recall when Grandma Dickson, Dad's
mom, and I first caught a glimpse of each other, but I
do know we developed a loving relationship as I was
growing up and she was an older woman with a limited
education and restricted economic possibilities.

Some sources have considered illiteracy as an
incurable disease. Functional illiteracy may be one step
above illiteracy but is certainly an ailment that discour-
ages, perhaps even prevents, individuals from participating successfully in society or the work world. The
functionally illiterate person does not possess reading
and writing skills beyond a very basic level.

Grandma Dickson was considered to be functionally illiterate. A widow from the time I remember,
she had great difficulty forming letters of the alphabet
when she tried to help me learn to read when I was age
four. I felt sorry for her and loved her very much for
her attempts, however simple.

Grandma Dickson's father had been an itinerant teacher, going from place to place on horseback to instruct youngsters in the rural areas of Arkansas. Unfortunately and ironically, he did not teach his own daughter to read or write.

The reason for her father's lack of attention to his daughter was never clear to me. There were rumors of an illegitimate birth, other rumors of an itinerant teacher so busy with other families' children that he had no time for his own offspring. Perhaps he didn't consider women worthy of an education. Whatever the truth, Grandma Dickson did not benefit from any type of formal or informal literacy training. The result was that she strove to function without the language tools needed to succeed.

While I cannot state with certainty that Grandma Dickson felt socially rejected because of her functional illiteracy, I am certain that she suffered from feelings of inadequacy in her attempt to manage her everyday life. She lived in one of the small cottages near the California pepper tree where I established my imaginary kingdom. She could see me from the windows of her cottage and perhaps watched me without my knowledge. She never interfered, however, with my imaginary exploits under the tree and gave me far more freedom to remain in my Pepper Tree Kingdom than my father would have done. She seemed to understand that I often needed to be alone with no intrusions.

Grandma Dickson grew up in the late 19th and early 20th centuries, long before the Baby Boomer generation and before women had gained the freedoms and possibilities they enjoy today. She was the grandmotherly type: chubby and the keeper of family quilts as well as chair and sofa coverings. She was "past-tense" oriented. Whether she was considered kind or harmful depended on whom you talked to.

I have no idea whether or not she really wanted to be a grandmother. If she did cherish her role, I doubt that she gave any thought to the type of grandmother she would be. She was raised during the period when "traditional grandmothers" were in vogue, but I never thought of her as such. Her values and roles seemed different in many ways from previous generations and even from her own generation. She worked at menial tasks outside the home. I do not remember her cooking as being outstanding even though she did prepare meals when the family got together in her small cottage. She seemed to have little enthusiasm for past wisdom even though she was past-oriented. She probably didn't have a clue about family stability or security. She had come from what seemed to be a dysfunctional family and had continued the dysfunctional tradition in her two marriages and child rearing. She may have distinguished between grandsons and granddaughters and probably preferred the grandsons. She seemed to have few, if any, family-first values.

Although it was not always evident, Grandma did possess what might be referred to as "grandmother goodness." When she could or wanted to do so, she gave precious time, considerable love and even everyday wisdom to me. She injected some simple playfulness into my humdrum life and a grain of needed stability.

Grandma Dickson seemed to be afraid of Dad but would go against his wishes, at least as far as I was concerned, when he was not around. She was the main person who encouraged me to venture from my kingdom and participate, even for short periods of time, in the real world.

Grandma's limited literacy kept her from even applying for a decent-paying position. As a result, she was very poor and cleaned both medical and dental offices to sustain herself. Several of the offices had to be cleaned early in the morning, a time when drug addicts and other individuals up to no good were roaming the streets of Wilmington. Sometimes the individuals even attempted to break into the offices while Grandma was there.

I can recall one morning in the early 1940s, when a man apparently high on something attempted to break down the door of one of the medical offices, hoping he could get hold of some drugs and possibly some money. He was breathing hard and moaning to himself, "I've got to get in."

Grandma and I waited patiently behind the door, which seemed to resist the man's attempted entry.

"Be very quiet," Grandma whispered. "He's probably very dangerous. If he thinks we're in here, he might try harder to get in."

I didn't answer or utter a sound.

We were both scared to death but refrained from making any noise until the door seemed unable to withstand the man's attack any further.

"You pretend to be the man cleaner," she whispered. "Make as much noise as you can."

I panicked. "I don't know where the mop is. Where did you put it?"

"It's in the waiting room. I'll get it for you."

Anxiety hit me as I slammed several doors. When we started making noises and carrying on our loud conversation, the man was apparently very surprised. He immediately stopped his attack on the door and disappeared. We waited a few minutes before opening another door to check on the man's whereabouts, but when we did check, we found no sign of a person, only the results of his attempt to enter: some wood splinters and many scratches and dents in the door and door frame.

After we called the doctor and the police and finished our cleaning tasks, Grandma attempted to explain what had happened.

"I didn't get to see the person who tried to get in, but I do know it was a man," she told the policeman who came to investigate the attempted entry. "He was talking to himself, sort of moaning. He was sure he could break down the door, and me and my grandson were scared. We thought he would kill us if he got in. So we made lots of noise to scare him off. It was an awful scary thing."

The policeman listened carefully but didn't answer. I think he was surprised that I was with Grandma Dickson as young as I was. He didn't ask me anything but did look me up and down. Apparently, he said something to the doctor because the doctor wanted to know if I accompanied Grandma Dickson very often, and I said, "Yes." Nothing else was said. No action was taken against Grandma Dickson for having me with her that early in the morning to help with the cleaning of the office even though I was very young. Both the doctor and the policeman must have understood that she needed help, and I was the only one she had available.

Grandma felt safer if I, a youngster of six or seven years of age, accompanied her to the offices, and so I would often get up around 3:30 to 4:00 a.m. and go with her. While she was cleaning, I would either do my homework or help her by dusting a desk or sweeping a floor. The time at the offices and the tasks involved allowed me to escape momentarily from my cocoon and brace myself for the coming day at school, but neither the time nor the tasks encouraged me to develop an identity that would allow me comfortably to interact with other youngsters or adults. I didn't mind rising early because I loved Grandma Dickson very much and realized that my presence meant a lot to her. I cherished the time with her and felt somewhat important since I made her feel a little more secure and safe.

One of the medical doctors for whom Grandma cleaned an office was the attending physician at my birth. He was an older man and loved to remind me that he had helped me come into this world. He was kind, gentle and understanding regarding any short-comings my grandmother or I might have had, but I could not identify with him. He had plenty of money and lived a type of life, even though relatively simple, that offered hope and security for the future. Even at this early age I saw the difference in the way my family lived and the doctor's way of life. I can't say I was jeal-ous, but I did feel insecure, particularly around the physician who seemed to have few, if any, financial worries. He lived in a lovely home in the more elite section of Wilmington and drove a beautiful car. He always dressed well. Whatever worries he might have had were well covered with images of prosperity and comfort.

The regular cleaning schedule, the brief interac-tion with the doctor and the attempted break-ins like the one involving the attack on the office door caused me anxiety. I didn't want to be a permanent member of the social group to which Grandma belonged, but I knew I could not easily be included in the group of which the doctor was a part.

A dentist whose office Grandma Dickson cleaned, however, managed to accomplish temporarily what none of the medical doctors was able to do: He helped me identify with him and briefly escape from my seclusion. The cleaning schedule for his office called for a late-afternoon arrival, just about the time he was closing the office and going home. As soon as he saw me, he would engage me in conversation and inquire about the condition of my teeth. He, in fact, pulled a baby tooth for me without charge and joked about how easily the tooth came out. That gesture really endeared him to me.

I particularly enjoyed the fuchsia plants that hung in the entrance to his office and on the patio next to the office. I loved the way the blossoms dangled from the stems like small bells hanging from delicate support systems. Also, I earned a little extra pocket money by watering the plants once or twice a week.

The verbal exchanges with the dentist that often took place while I was watering the plants were psychologically uplifting to me. He would stand near me while we chatted and I would gently direct the water to each potted fuchsia. Perhaps he wanted to make certain that I didn't give the plants too much or too little water. Whatever his purpose was in staying relatively close to me, I enjoyed the company. I looked forward to each conversation. For a brief few moments, I imagined an identity that pleased and uplifted me. Indirectly, and in my imagination, I temporarily became a part of his world.

But as soon as he left the area and my watering tasks were completed, I found myself slipping back into my cocoon and dreaming about my Pepper Tree Kingdom. I again began my search for who I was or who I could be. I quickly retreated into my psychological seclusion for protection and solace.

After several years of living in the two-room shanty bordering my Pepper Tree Kingdom, Grandma Dickson moved up the street to a four-room, detached cottage. By this time she had retired from her office-cleaning tasks and devoted much of her time to her quilting. Very often a quilting frame filled the living room of the cottage, and I had to make my way around the frame or crawl under the unfinished quilt to go from the living room to the kitchen.

The frame consisted of four substantial, pole-like wooden pieces. Two of the pieces would hold the width of the quilt while the other two pieces would enable Grandma to do her stitching. The patterns of the quilts varied but were all quite attractive.

Sometimes Grandma had what has been referred to as a "quilting bee." When she hosted such an event, her sister from one part of California and her cousin from another part of the state would be both be present. The three of them and sometimes local friends would quilt all day, stopping only long enough to have a bite of lunch or refreshments. Often those quilting sessions would continue for two or three days. In the evenings, the quilting frame would be lifted toward the ceiling but never dismantled. Grandma made certain that the quilters could resume their activities the next morning without delay.

Despite her functional illiteracy, Grandma Dickson seemed to sense my needs and made an effort to meet those needs to the extent she could. Even after my marriage, she would come to visit us and would enjoy going to various public places with us. I cannot recall the very last time I saw her, but I do remember talking with her once when I had come from Iran to visit Mother and Dad in Arkansas. During our conversation, Grandma asked me to visit her in Wilmington during my trip because, she said, she would not be around much longer and would love to see me once more before her death. I thought of taking the trip to California but for some reason did not. I was still at the age that death seemed far away, and I could not picture a loved one not being with me or not being available when I could make or wanted to pay a visit.

My gratitude to Grandma Dickson continues for the opportunities she afforded me to venture even temporarily from my cocoon and Pepper Tree Kingdom. I now realize more than I did as a child or even as a young adult the effort it took for her to do what little she could do for me. I also understand that the excursions I enjoyed because of her work did not lead to the establishment of an identity. The world she knew and in which she was forced to function never appealed to me, nor did I understand it. Her love and compassion for me are what I will always recall and be thankful for.

To me, Grandma Dickson represented a mom with lots of frosting. She blessed me in her homely way and was there when I needed her. She was beautiful inside and frequently demonstrated that beauty to me by letting me go to carnivals without telling my father or allowing me to ruminate for hours on my rope throne. She gave me freedom that I could have never enjoyed without her.

She was an antique little girl with limited possibilities, but she used those limited possibilities to help me. And I am eternally grateful to her for her efforts to lure me from my psychological isolation, even if each venture was short-lived.

Perhaps I can express my love and deep appreciation to Grandma Dickson for her concern for me and her feeble efforts to set me free by means of a simple poem, which I wrote years after Grandma's passing:

A Grandmother Like Grandma Dickson

I would just like to say, Grandma Dickson,
That you meant and continue to mean
so much to me.
In your simple and sometimes graceless way
You helped me learn how to be accepting.

You were often there
when I needed the support
That was not available at home
or from other sources.
I wish you had enjoyed a happier life
here on earth
But trust you are being treated well
in the heavenly court.

Chapter 6

>>>>))((<<<<

Two Generations in Conflict

Neither before nor following the death of my father, Jack, have I dreamt about him, but I have often pondered his motivation and relationship with me during my waking hours. I can still picture his sternness and cringe from fear. No bond existed between us. In most instances, our interactions were contentious and "hot as hell." I lived with Mother and Dad until my graduation from college at the age of twenty, and during that time and even for many years after establishing my own life, I was unable to find relief from the haunting sense of guilt Dad had instilled in me with his narrow approach to life and his almost "Old-Testament" way of correcting and chastening me.

I always wanted Dad to love me but never felt he did. At times, I felt that he viewed me as a means by which he could compensate for his rather sordid life. It seemed that he was determined to bind me to an altar of religious legalism without any promise of escape. He demanded that I observe the rites and ceremonies he created in accordance with what he viewed to be God's law and will. No movies. No parties. Little laughter. After all, laughter tended to lighten the atmosphere. He wanted to make sure I feared and worshipped God as he defined God. The severity of Dad's rules wreaked havoc on my psyche and self-esteem.

For years I have searched for recorded accounts of father-son relationships, and during that search I came across the nineteenth-century Russian novelist, short-story writer and playwright by the name of Ivan Turgenev. The title of one of Ivan Turgenev's novels is often translated into English as *Fathers and Children* or *Fathers and Sons*. It deals with the growing divide between two generations of Russians, the development of the philosophical doctrine of nihilism and the rejection of the established order, but its message can be applied to situations in which two generations develop different philosophies of life and simply grow apart because of their different orientations. The message certainly proved applicable to Dad and me.

Dad represented the narrow-minded conservatism of certain religious fanatics in rural Arkansas. He had experienced his religious epiphany during his mid-life years and after a rather colorful, some people would say debauched, existence, which included three marriages, two divorces, what I heard was considerable drinking and some uncertainty as to the lady with whom he would live after his marriage to Mother. A relative once confided that Dad returned to my half-brother's mother for a brief period before I was born but then decided to remain married to Mother. Exactly what took place remains a mystery, at least to me.

By the time I was old enough to understand what was transpiring, however, Dad had become almost a religious tyrant, motivated by adherence to his interpretation of Biblical truth and Christian dogma. He tolerated very little divergence from the message of Jesus as God and considered as revolutionary even those individuals who supported the practice of literal over spiritual communion.

Until I was about 10 years old, I followed Dad's religious lead and attempted to please him to the extent possible, but as I grew toward my teen years, I became what he considered a rebel or revolutionary. Pride in his "Jesus only" grasp of the godhead gave him a feeling of superiority, but the certainty with which he declared the doctrine turned me off and made me question the role of doctrine in Christianity. His feeling of pity toward Christians who believed in the Trinity made me question his grasp of Biblical teachings. Other religions were not even included in his spiritual landscape. If I considered a thought about religious doctrine that did not fit his mold, I was, in his opinion, out-of-line.

Any reference to baptism "in the name of the Father, Son and Holy Spirit" immediately drew negative comments from Dad. To him, the only legitimate baptismal seal was "in the name of Jesus."

Dad simply could not understand my decision to join the local Baptist church when I was fifteen. He totally avoided discussing the decision with me until the time he picked me up from a church event one mid-week night.

"I assume your church doesn't encourage young people to attend movies, does it?" he asked the pastor's wife.

"We leave the decision up to the individual or the family," the wife responded.

"At least you are not promoting sinful habits," Dad uttered.

"We try not to," the wife retorted.

At that point, the conversation ended, and Dad and I went on our way. Dad never complained to me about my decision, but through such short conversations as the one with the pastor's wife and questions he would ask about the church, I knew he felt I had made a mistake in veering away from his accepted religious path.

In Turgenev's novel the two characters Paul Petrovich and Bazarov battle philosophically over the future of the Russian culture; as I entered my teen years, Dad and I fought endlessly, sometimes subtly and often very openly, over the foundation and future of religion. The contrast in our views represented not only a generation gap but a rejection, at least in part, by me of Dad's view of an acceptable existence. Dad early on developed the attitude that I was attempting to destroy a way of life that had brought him out of the pits of social degradation.

Many psychologists suggest that fathers should not judge or command but guide and nurture their sons in the development of a meaningful father-son relationship. The relationship must include honesty, openness, communication, acceptance and respect on the part of the father toward the son. The role of the father at times requires expressions of understanding when the son may disagree.

Dad unfortunately never seemed to care whether or not he could become a father figure, nor did he seem to desire a strong father-son relationship. Seldom, if ever, did he show an understanding of or interest in even the simplest of my ideas. Never did he attend a high school function or college function with me. Despite the invitations, he didn't attend my high school or college graduation.

He had a commanding approach to raising me with a total lack of two-way communication, consolation or respect. It was not unusual for him to say something to the effect, "I wish that was true. Does the Bible really say that? I'm not sure that is what the Bible says."

He believed he was always right; my way of looking at a situation or scripture or the interpretation of another individual was not acceptable unless it met his religious and socially conservative criteria. No matter how much I attempted to create and promote a respectful and open-communication environment, he refused to budge from his opinions or consider my ideas. To him, the only way was his way, at least until late in his life.

In addition to Dad's tendency to be fixed in his ways and ideas was his absence from home for sometimes weeks at a time. Evangelistic campaigns were among his favorite means of escape, and he didn't seem to view the campaigns as a means of supporting the family. His purpose seemed of a higher nature: the spreading of his version of the Christian gospel. These absences, I now understand, kept him from serving in such capacities at home as moral overseer, nurturing parent and even a trustworthy breadwinner. He forewent his role in the family for what he considered the broader and more important task of saving souls.

During my childhood and much of my teen years, Dad's frequent absences from home plus his stubbornness had extremely negative effects on my social and psychological development. I was always unsure of myself and had no confidence in my own ideas. I performed well in school but remained psychologically maladjusted and extremely antisocial. I had very few dates with the opposite sex in high school and experienced considerable difficulty in establishing and continuing any type of intimate relationship. I took solace in my academic studies and western-popular music study and performance.

I avoided parties at almost any cost, and even when the relatives gathered for a reunion, I would be reluctant to attend. I loved performing but didn't enjoy the interaction with members of the audience after a show or wedding ceremony.

Ernest Hemingway wrote a story, "Fathers and Sons," which involved a father by the name of Nick and his son. The two return to Nick's hometown and Nick becomes aware that few things in the town are the same as they were when he was a child. Suddenly he awakens to the fact that he needs to create a positive memory of his father by becoming a better father to his son.

When I was six years old, Dad returned from California to Hot Springs, Arkansas, his hometown. He, however, didn't share Nick's concerns or attempt to improve in his role as a father figure. He offered little orientation to Hot Springs, enrolled me in a segregated school some distance from the home he rented for us and soon focused on his evangelistic endeavors. After two years he returned to California.

The move to Hot Springs and the return to California were not our only changes of residency. Dad loved to move from place to place and very often. Back in California from Arkansas, he first moved to Wilmington, then to Riverside, from there to Pomona and finally back to Wilmington. All of the towns were in California but quite a distance apart.

Some of the moves, I believe, were related to his work, but often they seemed mere attempts to create new situations, both financially and spiritually. Most of the efforts were not successful either spiritually or financially and left Mother and me increasingly alone.

Several of the attempts to bring about a more stable financial situation involved the raising of animals. I can recall one time in Hot Springs when Dad had bought and installed Mother and me in a home without electricity or running water. He decided he would raise chickens on the property for extra income and purchased several hens and roosters. The experiment in chicken farming went well for the first few weeks, but his frequent absences meant that Mother and I inherited the task of feeding and caring for the creatures. One night, sometime in early winter, the weather turned cold and damp. A heavy rain ensued, and several of the chickens drowned. Dad wasn't happy with the result of his chicken experiment, but he couldn't say much since he was not around to perform the tasks necessary to save the animals.

A second experiment in raising animals at a temporary residence was carried out in Wilmington, when Dad bought a goat for the purpose of providing our family with goat milk. He kept the goat in the backyard of the rented home. The house was, incidentally, in the center of town, and I don't know how he obtained, or if he did obtain, permission to have the animal around. At any rate, the goat fared well for several months until Dad decided to feed him the clover that had grown up in the backyard. The goat was fine the night he was given the clover but was dead the next morning. His stomach had bloated and practically burst. Only then did we learn that goats were allergic to the type of grass growing in the yard.

Dad's only potentially successful experiment in animal husbandry was conducted in Riverside, California, and I ruined that experiment for him. The Riverside home was in a rather rural area where small animals could be raised without difficulty. For some reason, Dad decided to breed and raise rabbits both for food and sale. I enjoyed the company of the rabbits very much and fed and watered them without fail. The difficulty arose when Dad wanted to kill one of them. The rabbits had become my friends, and I could not entertain the thought of one of them being slaughtered and eaten. Dad overrode my concern for a while but finally gave up the idea of creating any capital through the marketing of rabbit meat.

I never really felt Dad accepted me for who and what I was and wanted me to be more like his image of an ideal Christian youth. His image required attendance at church three or four times each week, no movies, only parties with youth from a church rather than from a school, no dancing at parties, no close contact between boys and girls. He was sure that personal rather than group interaction between boys and girls would generally lead to the commitment of "sins."

Dad finally began to show some flexibility after Mahin and I got married. At first, he was against the marriage. Mahin represented another religion and a "foreign" culture, but she soon won him over. I have long thought that he came to love her even more than he ever loved me. I am thankful for that though and will always relish the relationship he and Mother were able to develop with Mahin.

I don't recall Dad ever embracing me or offering to help me in any way, but I happily remember when Mahin had experienced a situation that had led to a visit to a physician and a temporary loss of strength. Mother and Dad met Mahin and me outside our apartment after our visit to the doctor, and Dad saw how weak Mahin really was. Without saying a word, he picked her up and carried her up a flight of stairs to our second-floor apartment. Then he carefully set her on a sofa and made sure she was comfortable. He beamed with pride that he had been able to help her. I was pleasantly surprised to see a different side of Dad—a warmer side I was never on the receiving end of.

Proof that Mother and Dad held Mahin in high esteem showed in their only trip abroad: to Iran. When they let me know they were coming to visit us in Tehran, I was surprised and puzzled, but they arrived within a few weeks and stayed for some ten days.

While in Tehran, Dad participated in cocktail hours and interacted easily with Mahin's brothers and other members of the family. I regretted that he and I were able to enjoy each other for such a short period of time. He experienced health problems not too long after their return to the United States and passed away before I could leave Iran and arrive in Hot Springs, where he and Mother had again moved after he was unable to work anymore.

Dad was not physically abusive nor did he physically abandon me, but he did abandon me psychologically and at times made life quite miserable for me. In many ways, I believe his inflexibility motivated me to become more tolerant and accepting of a multiplicity of ideas. I didn't want to live the unrewarding life I felt he lived and even forced Mother at times to live. My marriage to Mahin and her willingness to tolerate my lack of social skills and her ability to tutor me in developing lasting relationships saved me from isolation and ultimate total introversion.

The passage of time has softened my resentment toward Dad. His approach to religion may have stifled my social development, but it did instill in me a deep appreciation for spiritual matters. His rigidity, I now realize, encouraged me to develop a willingness to listen to and consider a variety of ideas. Intellectual rigidity has long been anathema to me.

In retrospect, I now feel Dad meant well and staunchly believed his extremely religious, even legalistic, approach to child rearing would result in a better adjusted and understanding son. While I cannot readily accept or appreciate his approach to developing a father-son relationship, I do feel he sincerely had my best interest at heart. Further, resentment toward him now hurts only me and tends to mar my happiness. He has gone to be with God and is probably more relaxed and hopefully more forgiving. I look forward to meeting him after my journey here on earth has been completed.

Chapter 7

>>>))(((<<

Seen But Not Heard

Mother's frail, ninety-one-year-old body lay on her small bed in the nursing home in Hot Springs, breathing heavily and unable to recognize me. I struggled with the reality of her condition and the acceptance of the inevitability of her impending death. I wanted to cry but couldn't. Memories of her unexpressed love for me and the many questions I had long wanted to ask her about our relationship came flooding back into my consciousness.

If only she had expressed her love to me openly. I knew she loved me; after all, I was her only remaining child. Her daughter, Barbara, had died at birth, and she had had me some three years later. I never heard of another pregnancy. It seemed, however, she could only hint at her love for me. I don't remember hearing her tell me she cared for me. Many times she intimated her love but could not seem to make herself utter the phrase "I love you." She would cooperate with Grandma Dickson in sneaking me to carnivals against Dad's orders and never utter a word to him. She would attend school and college functions and would beam with happiness when I would receive an award or be recognized for my scholastic efforts. She would sometimes ask to go to church with me and would apparently enjoy every minute she spent with me. It seemed she loved to go out to lunch with me, particularly on Sundays.

If only she had voiced her frustration with Dad when he made his dictatorial announcements concerning both her and me and demanded that I accept his rigidity without question or experience his verbal retaliation. I watched her closely on many occasions and detected frustration. Her slim body would tense up. Her eyebrows would arch, and tears would well up in her eyes but seldom fell to her cheeks. She would sit for long periods of time without uttering a word. Sometimes her hands would shake just enough to encourage her to grab the arms of the chair or sofa she happened to be lounging on. She would appear frail and unnerved.

I would listen for Mother's retorts to Dad's demands but never heard any. Her tongue seemed tied, her ability to contradict Dad or attempt to reason with him nonexistent. She sometimes had the appearance, at least to me, of a psychologically battered wife or a wife who had accepted a fate that offered no means of easy escape.

If only I could have discovered what she had wanted to do with her life before Dad entered the picture and why she had been so faithful to Dad even when, I understand, he left her temporarily to attempt reconciliation with his first wife.

If only she had been able, to paraphrase author Elizabeth Stone, to walk her heart around outside her body. She had a heart of gold, never gossiped and always spoke well of others. She was the type who would wave to me each time I would pass her on a merry-go-round. But that was about as far as she could go emotionally.

I have read that some psychologists believe mothers teach boys how to love and trust. Boys become emotionally and psychologically stronger because of their mothers' love. They feel free to explore and develop courage as a result of the mother-son connection. Boys learn self-respect when their mothers provide a safe and secure home base. Mother did nothing to make me feel insecure, but neither did she attempt to offer safety against Dad's unreasonable demands and expectations. I think that, like Grandma Dickson, Mother feared Dad even though he was not physically abusive to her. She didn't want his psychological retribution.

Mothers who have to raise their sons alone or with little support from husbands may make the sons the father figure or insist on the sons becoming mama's boys. Mother did neither.

Sons may be made to feel insecure if mothers have had their own attachment issues in childhood and cannot develop close relationships with their sons. In short, the mothers may project their lack of connection on to their sons, thereby perpetuating the lack of attachment and sense of identity. Perhaps Mother's attachment to her grandfather rather than her mother and father discouraged her from bonding with me.

Mother was the eldest of four children, the only daughter. Her mother, in poor health from my Mother's early childhood, allowed Mother's grandparents to raise her. I recall Mother becoming nostalgic about her grandfather, but there was never any mention of a close relationship. She was proud of his Masonic background and the fact that he had served as the official surveyor of the territory that later became the State of Arkansas. When I became a Mason in the 1980s, Mother proudly gave me her grandfather's Masonic pin. This gesture, I believe, proved her love for me.

I do not recall that Mother ever discussed her mother except to say that she had become very ill and had died when she and Mother's father, Grandpa Robbins, were on their way from Arkansas to California. The death occurred in Mesa, Arizona, and the mother was apparently buried there. Grandpa Robbins continued his immigration from Arkansas to "the promised land" of Southern California, leaving his recently buried wife behind never to return to the grave—or so I've heard.

Whether Mother felt any attachment to her father I never knew. I did not get to know Grandpa Robbins until he had lived in Bishop, California for a number of years. Mother and I took the Greyhound bus from downtown Los Angeles to Bishop two or three times during my childhood and stayed for several days with Grandpa Robbins and Mother's brothers, all three of whom lived in Bishop at the time.

I was six or seven when we took the bus trips, and the most disturbing incidents that took place during those trips involved the Japanese and their incarceration.

After the bombing of Pearl Harbor in 1941, President Franklin Roosevelt asked Congress to declare war on the Japanese, and many of the Japanese residents in the United States were incarcerated in camps in several locations in the United States. By 1943, the United States was fully engaged in World War II.

The Greyhound that we boarded for the trips would make its way up Highway 395 and stop along the way. One of the stops was at the Manzanar War Location Center, where the U.S. Government had collected hundreds, perhaps thousands, of Japanese farmers and small business owners who lived and worked in California. When we stopped at the camp gate, I could see the temporary barracks and the communal areas for bathing, doing the laundry and eating. Internees would be leaning against or peering through barbed-wire fences, silently begging to be released, given adequate medical care and offered relief from the temperature extremes. The military personnel stood at attention with their guns at their sides. To this day, desolate images flash through my mind, and the memory sears my conscience.

From the War Location Center, the bus would take us on to Bishop where Mother went with mixed feelings and few expectations. She merely tolerated one of her brothers, Ernest, but got on well with two of them: Garland, who recently passed way at 101 years of age and Lawrence, the youngest who died at an early age of lung cancer. The brothers later dispersed, and I don't remember seeing them together after our few visits to Bishop.

Speaking of tolerating each other, one thing always remained a mystery to me—Mother's attraction to Dad. She never revealed why she decided to marry him, but I sometimes felt it was because of her naiveté about men, her limited background in dating the opposite sex and her desire for companionship. After two marriages and one child by each wife plus, what might have been several love affairs, Dad was certainly worldlier than was Mother when they met.

I never understood whether Mother feared Dad or whether she simply didn't have the fortitude to challenge him when he enforced his demands on us. When I was a child, and Dad insisted on my attendance at church, Mother never objected to his strong command even though she herself seldom attended church with us. She either feared him or wanted to avoid conflict at all cost. The reason for her not expressing her feelings or objections in relation to Dad was never clear.

During my early school years in Wilmington, Mother cleaned offices for extra money. I can't remember whether she obtained the jobs through Grandma Dickson and her contacts, but she was a hard worker. One day while on the job, she fell and broke her arm and was incapacitated for a period of time. She remained in our small apartment for several weeks but never uttered a complaint or grievance about her condition or the fact that she was alone most of the time. She never expressed her feelings. But I don't believe she ever really recovered from the break or the period of isolation. The memory of her fall, her isolation and weakness flashed back as I watched her on her deathbed. It seemed her health deteriorated gradually from the time of her fall, even though she lived for some fifty years after.

Mother attended both my high school and college graduation ceremonies and appeared happy to do so. She didn't mind having her photograph taken. She was even present at our older daughter Ladan's high school graduation. Never in any of the ceremonies, however, do I recall her saying, "Congratulations. I am proud of you for your accomplishments," or a similar sentence of encouragement. I would have given much to have her congratulate me on anything I had accomplished, but she was either too shy to say the words or perhaps didn't take pride in my accomplishments. I have long hoped it was the former.

It was not until toward the end of her life that I saw Mother show her emotions. I don't recall her ever crying until she was in her eighties. Perhaps she did shed tears at times, but she successfully suppressed her emotions until late in her life. Only when I visited her after Dad's death did I become aware of her emotional side. Even then when she was sharing her sadness, she seemed more comfortable opening her feelings to others than to me.

I'm sure that Mother had a story to tell about her childhood and lack of attachment. She must have had memories and tales regarding her mother. Certainly, her father was in her life for many years. I have, however, long felt that her grandfather was her life-giver. The grandfather appeared to be more the nurturer than the grandmother.

I looked up to Mother not with wonder and awe but with questions and concern. Her apparent timidity in relation to Dad and her inability to express an opinion concerned me. I wanted my Mother to be a strong individual with whom I could interact on a fair basis and enjoy support in times of need, but I settled for a wonderful person who was always present but never heard.

Much of my earlier life consisted of a journey with Mother, but the two of us never became intimate life-travel partners. My mother figure presented herself when I moved to Iran and became acquainted with Mahin's mother, *Khanim Jan*. Almost from the time of our introduction, I felt I had someone who would support me the way I had always wanted Mother to help me.

If Mahin and I had even a small disagreement, *Khanim Jan* would ask that Mahin carefully consider my opinion. She would often say, "Frank seems to have a good point. Why can't we at least think carefully about what he is suggesting?"

She would also make certain that either she or the servants would prepare the food she knew I really liked. Many times I heard her tell the cook, "Frank likes lentil soup. Let's prepare that for lunch. Make sure it's ready when he arrives at noon from the university." She seemed to support me with ease and determination. She, along with Mahin, helped me gain considerable confidence.

Pablo Picasso's mother encouraged him from childhood to become the best in whatever endeavor he undertook. She would tell him that if he became a soldier, he would eventually become a general or if he became a monk, he would eventually end up as the pope. Picasso, of course, became a very famous painter. He entered and excelled in a field which his mother had not considered or about which she probably knew little; he succeeded in his field, at least to an extent, because of his mother's consistent encouragement and prompting. I longed for such support or even a show of faith in my ability from Mother, but, alas, it wasn't meant to be.

Mother seemed more like a chaperone than a parent or role model. At her bedside as she lay dying, however, I looked down at her pale face, then looked heavenward and whispered, "Forgive me for any resentment I have for Mother's lack of support."

I searched myself and murmured another short prayer: "God, please forgive both Mother and me for not being able to make a better connection in this life. Help us to connect better in the next life."

I then bade Mother *adieu*. I felt certain that we would meet sometime in the future in God's presence where no encouragement is needed and no resentment exists. I commended her to God's care and sought to feel the bond in imminent death that I had longed for but had never felt in life.

Mother wasn't the typical mom. She had always been frail and had suffered from osteoporosis. But, as I look back now, I realize that she must have had a very strong character to have put up with some of Dad's outlandish demands without threatening to leave or respond negatively. The strength, however, often appeared to be a weakness. Her personality seemed flawed despite her strength. I left the nursing home as confused as ever about Mother who was usually present but never heard and who didn't help me discover who I was or could be.

As I recalled Mother's silence for the many years I lived at home and indirectly begged for her support, I had an epiphany: God had given me, in the form of a wife, the person I had needed and wanted all my life. To this day, I'm not sure what first encouraged Mahin to accept my invitation to go on a date. She once told me that she saw potential in me that I did not see in myself, but so many young men were attracted to Mahin and were seeking her companionship that her willingness to join with me in life's journey remains somewhat a joyful mystery. Perhaps it was a match made in heaven. Whatever the attraction was, it was mutual and eternally remains so.

Chapter 8

>>>))((<<<

Bullying:
Its Role in My Search for an Identity

When I was eight years old, what proved to be the catalyst for finding myself appeared in the most unlikely of circumstances. The auditorium was packed with students called together for an all-school program at my elementary school in Wilmington. Seated between two hefty specimens of masculinity, I worried a bit about my size, stature and physique in relation to theirs.

The program got underway, and after a few announcements, we stood for the pledge of allegiance. When we had completed the pledge, I tried to sit down but realized something was piercing the right cheek of my butt.

"Why don't you sit down?" one of the boys asked laughingly. "You can't stand during the program."

I didn't answer. A sharp pain had set in. I attempted to stand up straight but encountered a strong resistance from both sides. The two beefcakes laughed and forced me to a seated position; it was then that I realized that something had been placed between my butt and the seat, and that something was the cause of my discomfort.

I suffered the pain until the end of the program but finally went to the boys' bathroom to discover why my butt was hurting so badly. Although I couldn't see the object clearly, I could tell something was embedded in the skin. I soon learned it was the lead of a sharp pencil.

For several days I suffered pain and confusion, but I never reported the incident to the school principal, my teacher or even my parents. I thought the principal would think I was a wimp, and the teacher hadn't paid much attention to me. I was sure Dad would say, "Can't you take care of yourself?" Mother would never offer a word of support if Dad didn't respond positively.

Neither one of the bullies threatened retribution if I reported the incident, but I was afraid that the instigators might take revenge on me if I squealed on them to the school administrators. Certainly, I didn't welcome sarcastic remarks from Dad or any more trouble than I already had with the incident and the developing wound. I felt keeping my mouth shut was my best line of defense. The wound gradually healed, and the pencil lead worked its way out of my skin. Lead in the cheek of the butt is an experience one never forgets.

For the remainder of the academic year, I didn't follow a daily routine at school or allow myself the pleasure of being alone on the playground. I constantly looked around and sneaked from one place to another even when other students were nearby. The incident had launched me on a journey of fear and anxiety, and I was not certain how to manage that tyranny or bring it to a halt. I wanted to find out why the two boys hurt me, but I never had the courage to ask them. Finally, I convinced myself the incident had occurred because of who I was to them: a weak, vulnerable creature subconsciously asking to be demeaned and bullied.

Although I did experience a few additional episodes of physical harassment or bullying, on most occasions the bullying was psychological, subtle and indirect. In elementary school, captains never chose me when they were selecting their athletic team members or when their teams were competing against other teams. Quite often, I sat on a bench and watched the athletes demonstrate their prowess. Both inside and outside the classroom, few students attempted to cultivate my friendship. I was usually the odd man out.

I carried the stigma of shame and weakness because I was short in stature, small-boned but chubby. I moved with a slow pace and was a bit clumsy.

In high school, I chose to participate in what was then termed "corrective gym." My Portuguese instructor was very understanding. During each class, he led me and several other classmates through a series of exercises designed to correct our posture and improve our overall strength. Even though he was a coach, he never mentioned competitive athletics to us and refrained from asking why we didn't attempt to participate in team activities. He knew the reason for our lack of interest in athletics and physical competition: We were afraid to show our inability in competitive sports and felt unworthy of participation in competitive games.

The attitudes I correctly or incorrectly perceived others held toward me affected me negatively, and I gradually assumed a self-bullying approach to my own existence. I felt that I couldn't perform any task well or was not intelligent enough to accomplish anything. I thought I deserved the criticism that I so hated and feared. I developed a perfectionist approach that allowed me to be overly critical of myself when I did not meet my own expectations. I got to the point that I would criticize everything I did even when someone else complimented me on what I had done. I became my own worst enemy without realizing what I was doing to myself.

Despite my tendency to kiss myself off, Mahin saw something in me that I had never seen in myself: academic possibilities and an undeveloped love for people and other cultures. Well into my marriage, I gradually developed a different attitude toward myself. I began to enjoy some positive comments about my accomplishments and behavior. I allowed myself to observe my feelings. Timidly, I began to defend myself by expressing my opinions and gently challenging the opinions of others when I felt those opinions were without reason or unsupportable. I slowly found that self-defense sometimes yielded positive results. After several years, I was able to stop comparing myself to everyone else and could stand in front of a mirror and acknowledge who I was. I could, at least to an extent, be myself.

During my childhood and teenage years, bullying seemed to be a part of growing up; today people are asking why bullying has to be a part of the maturation process. More and more people are declaring that youngsters don't have to experience intimidation or mental anguish. I wish people had felt that way when I was experiencing physical and mental harassment.

Without the bullying, perhaps I could have left my self-imposed exile from much of society earlier in life and enjoyed myself sooner and advanced professionally more than I have. I possibly could have become the attorney Mahin always wanted me to be.

Mahin encouraged me and broadened my perspectives through her insistence on attending movies, musicals and travel. She made sure I met friends who held important positions in the Government of Iran, international organizations like the United Nations and contractors with the U.S. Department of State. It was not, however, until Mahin and I had been married for several years that I felt I was intelligent enough to contribute to an intellectual conversation or interpret what was happening around me.

Today, I don't worry about psychological torment or bullying. Having lifted the burden of worry and self-torment from my shoulders, I can participate in life and enjoy my social as well as my professional activities. I continue more easily and happily to become my full self, enjoying my own company more and more, being increasingly able to listen to and empathize with my fellow human beings and living life to the fullest, searching for greater understanding and enjoying what each day brings.

Chapter 9

>>>>>>>>>>(((((((<<

Spiritual Hopscotch

The game of hopscotch represents a vestige of a pre-Christian ritual, which the Christian Church transformed into a children's game. The word "hopscotch" represents a combination of two words: "hop" and the old French word *"escocher,"* which means "cut or scratch."

Hopscotch evolved in Britain during the Roman Period. The Roman military believed the game would improve the footwork of the soldiers and developed hopscotch courts that were more than one hundred feet long.

The game can be played alone or with others and begins with a marker that is tossed from outside the hopscotch court into the first square. The marker must land in the square without touching a line or bouncing out. Each player begins at square one and proceeds through the court and back to the starting line.

In my opinion, the game has many of the same characteristics as the spiritual journey. Each spiritual sojourner tosses his/her marker, the spiritual identity, into the first square of the spiritual-hopscotch court from outside the court and hopes that the marker does not land on a line or bounce out. The sojourner wants the result of the throw to be clear and without complication.

With each throw of the marker, the identity may change and will probably be completely different by the time the spiritual player looks back at the starting line to review his/her progress and ultimately has to return to the starting line.

From childhood I have been fascinated by Aimee Semple McPherson and her game of spiritual hopscotch. Often referred to as Sister Aimee, her game and experiences seemed to mirror mine, or vice-versa. She lived and functioned in a somewhat earlier era, but the similarities in backgrounds were notable.

Founder of the Foursquare Church, officially termed the International Church of the Foursquare Gospel, Sister Aimee was exposed to religion through her mother. My exposure came primarily through my father. Her mother was active in the Salvation Army, Dad in the "Jesus Only" movement. She became a well-known faith healer; Dad attempted to promote me as a healer also even though I never felt I had the gift of healing.

Incidentally, while both the "Jesus Only" movement and the Foursquare Church, are Pentecostal denominations, considerable differences in belief separate the two. A major difference is the view of the Godhead. The name of the "Jesus Only" movement clearly indicates that the Triune God does not exist in the opinions of adherents to that movement. Jesus is God and no other part of the Godhead should be acknowledged. The Foursquare Church accepts the doctrine of the Trinity.

Ms. McPherson played church as a child, as did I. Frequently, I would pretend to gather an imaginary congregation in my Pepper Tree Kingdom or another quiet place and preach sermons to the attendees. When I wasn't preaching, I was teaching either about religious matters or topics I was studying in school. Unlike Ms. McPherson, I never dwelled on Darwin's Theory of Evolution. I accepted Creationism as the gospel and did not even consider the possibility of reconciling the two points-of-view until later in life.

When she became a teenager, Sister Aimee defied her mother's teachings as well as those of the Salvation Army by reading novels, attending movies and going to dances. Like Sister Aimee, I rebelled against the strict teachings of the religious movement of which Dad was a part early in my teens and read all kinds of novels and even went to movies. I never, however, learned to dance despite the efforts of a number of friends and acquaintances.

Sister Aimee often asked pastors about religious topics of interest to her and was usually disappointed with the answers she received. I seldom received responses to my questions that satisfied my curiosity.

Ultimately, Sister Aimee settled in Los Angeles and collected sufficient funds to build a large church known as Angeles Temple in the Echo Park area of the city. It was to this building and the services held there that my parents would go and take me with them.

In the area of faith healing, however, our experiences differed considerably. Sister Aimee enjoyed the reputation of a faith healer but did not emphasize that gift. It remained somewhat incidental to her attempt at spreading the Foursquare Gospel through the use of modern media.

Dad made every effort to ensure that faith healing was one of my gifts. I appreciated his attempts to enhance my spirituality and supposed gift for helping others in physical distress, but my interests lay more in religious music and its capability to influence individuals and groups toward the acceptance of Christianity.

An example of Dad's determination to make me a faith healer occurred when I was only nine years old. The setting was a modest home in downtown Los Angeles; the crowd was small. The stakes, however, seemed very high: Dad had introduced me as a possible "faith healer," and individuals asked me to pray for them in the hope that through me God would rid them of their ailments and handicaps. One attendee couldn't walk; another reportedly suffered from an advanced stage of cancer. Each one of the people present had a significant health problem. There must have been between fifteen and twenty men and women with major handicaps who were seeking relief from their suffering. Crutches and wheelchairs crowded the room.

For a nine-year-old youngster the pressure was great. I realized that I was the center of attention, not because of me but because of what people expected God to do through me. I didn't feel I had any particular supernatural power or could serve as a conduit for God's healing power, but I did not want to disappoint Dad or the small crowd. What could I do? My decision was to make every effort to pray effectively for those present while attempting to discover a way to avoid any further complications or involvement in such gatherings. During that particular healing session, I came to realize that Dad was, through me, attempting to overcome what he viewed as his shortcomings. His attempt brought unbelievable pressure on me. The pressure caused reluctance and ambivalence toward my role as "healer."

My hands would shake as I placed them on the head of an expectant seeker of healing. I faltered in my prayers and sometimes stopped to ask for God's grace and intervention. While praying for the seekers, I couldn't sit but could hardly stand. My legs would tremble, and my knees would nearly buckle.

"Dear God," I prayed. "Please help me to get through this exercise. I promise I will not let Dad put either You or me in this position again."

My decision to engage while actually disengaging was typical of my childhood behavior, both in my religious and non-religious life. This dichotomous attitude became my approach to most situations and activities early on, and the attempt to affect some type of miracle through my personal connection with God frightened me greatly, making my tendency to disengage even stronger. The effort to mold me into a faith-healer intensified my distrust as well as dislike of what might be viewed as religious or spiritual showmanship.

Sister Aimee practiced speaking in tongues but did not emphasize the practice. Her reputation as a faith healer became less important in her ministry as she became increasingly famous. She believed in and preached the Triune God: the Father, Son and Holy Spirit. She may have been somewhat unorthodox in some of her practices and approach to religion, but she didn't cast the traditional doctrines totally aside.

Dad was different and wanted me to be different. He scoffed at those who took communion and those professing to believe in the Triune God. To him, Jesus was God. There was no other. While growing up, I often wondered how many of the Trinity would actually be in heaven if and when I arrived there.

My inability to discover a stable spiritual identity discouraged me from proceeding to the next square in my game of spiritual hopscotch and certainly deterred me from returning to the beginning square to examine my spiritual progress or lack thereof. Only in recent years have I begun to advance by seeking God's will for my life through studying the Bible with an open mind for spiritual revelation, prayer, meditation and an attitude of surrender to the will of God.

Chapter 10

>>>>>)((((<<

Vision or Apparition?
Supernatural Experiences

The word supernatural evokes strong emotion
in me, particularly since my childhood involved attempts to present me as a faith healer and the posses-
sor of possible powers I neither understood nor felt I
had. The term has often frightened but has always intrigued me. I relate it to spirituality, which can lift me
from the material world to the non-material realm.

Since childhood, I have frequently felt a guardi-
an spirit hovering over or near me. I have never been
able to explain the phenomenon even to myself but
have accepted the non-visual presence. Often, when I
am praying or meditating, I can picture a stream of water falling from space into my hands and on my body;
the water seems to invigorate me. I have even been
able to picture a physical being sitting somewhere in
the universe pouring the water out of a huge earthen
jar with a gentle, reassuring smile on his face.

But four specific experiences have strongly affected my relationship to the supernatural and acceptance of an unexplainable world beyond my current
existence. Three of the experiences might be called either apparitions or visions because they possessed
characteristics of both phenomena. If referred to as

visions, they would be "corporeal visions." All three were characterized by the disembodiment of a deceased family member but boasted the human head, as it existed in life. There was no material stimulus and the three took place totally without human assistance.

The fourth experience could probably be categorized only as a vision, taking place in broad daylight through a small bird. Some critics might contend that the latter merely represented a strong imagination.

The three apparitions/visions must have involved supernatural agents because no person was with me at the time. I was reluctant to admit they were related to real beings.

The first occurred when I was approximately seventeen. I was living in Wilmington, California, and my maternal grandfather, who I believe was in his late seventies, was a resident of Bishop, California. Mother had gone to visit her father, having heard he was ill, but I was not aware his illness was fatal. I thought he would survive and be with us at least a few years longer.

On the Saturday morning at approximately 7:00 a.m., following Mother's departure for Bishop, I was lying in my bed planning my day. The weather was mild and the sun shone brightly. My room was well lit and I was fully awake.

Suddenly, my grandfather appeared at the foot of my bed. His face was brilliant, his hair revealed the beautiful white color I had known from early childhood. From his neck down, he shown with radiance I had never seen before but had heard about in Biblical stories like the conversion of Saint Paul on his way to Damascus.

I was so stunned at Grandfather's appearance that I was unable to say anything. He continued to stand at the foot of my bed for two or three minutes before he said anything.

"I came to say goodbye. I left this world earlier this morning and wanted to make certain I let you know that I am all right. I will miss you but hope to see you again someday in the next world."

Immediately after completing his short monologue, he disappeared. I lay back on my pillows for a few more minutes, not knowing exactly what to do. Finally, I was able to pull myself together and call Mother in Bishop. That call revealed that Grandfather had passed on earlier that morning. His passing had been calm and quiet. He apparently had been ready for the transition from this earth to a heavenly existence. For many years, I didn't reveal my vision of Grandfather and the message he personally delivered to me. I feared listeners and friends would think I had lost my mind and label me a misfit.

I had the second experience while living in Iran during the early 1970s which involved my precious Mother-in-Law, respectfully and lovingly referred to as *Khanim Jan* or "Dear Lady." *Khanim Jan* lived in the heart of Tehran, and Mahin and I were living in Northern Tehran.

Khanim Jan had been ill for several days, and her condition did not seem to be improving. Both Mahin and I had been visiting with her during the day; toward evening, I decided to go to our home and rest for awhile. The time was approximately 8:00 p.m., and I was again resting in my bed with my eyes open. I couldn't fall asleep. Suddenly I glanced toward the foot of my bed and discovered *Khanim Jan*'s brilliant face. Her piercing eyes were looking straight at me. Her gray hair looked perfectly natural. I stared at her for a minute or two and then inquired, in Farsi, "*Khanim Jan*, do you have a message for me?"

For several seconds, she didn't respond to my question and her lack of response made me quite nervous. My nervousness prompted me to ask her a perhaps ill-advised question:

"What is beyond the low barrier I can see between us?" I asked.

Khanim Jan's face remained calm, but she responded in Farsi, "I don't think you should ask questions right now. Just enjoy my presence for a few minutes. This may be the last time you can experience me in this form."

Her apparent reluctance to discuss what the other side of the low barrier was like perplexed me, and I didn't wait to hear whatever message she had for me.

"I must know what lies beyond that barrier. I must know."

She hesitated but finally advised, "Please don't insist on discovering something you can't really know at this point."

I attempted to reach beyond the barrier. When I made my move, she again advised me, "Do not insist on learning about things that may be impossible for you to understand right now."

I made one additional effort to reach across the barrier, and when I did her image began to disappear. Then, I knew she was departing from me, and I hadn't yet discovered anything about the other world, nor had I let her deliver whatever message she had for me.

"I am all right. I am now in a better place," she whispered in Persian as her image faded. That was all she wanted me to know. A telephone call revealed that she had passed on only a few minutes before her appearance in our bedroom.

My third experience occurred during a Saturday-night service in a small church in Concord, California. The pastor was discussing the power of God and His blessings; suddenly my deceased wife and a pastor, with whom I had served at Walnut Creek Presbyterian Church and who had just passed on, appeared to me. Neither one had the cloudy image of the first two apparitions, but their faces were as clear as if it were a sunny day. The faces of both were just as they had been while they were here on earth, but I could not detect any other parts of their bodies. The two were seemingly sitting or standing across from each other and laughing heartily. They both looked my way but said nothing. They continued to honor me with their smiles for almost a minute. From my experience during the second apparition I knew not to begin asking questions. I merely enjoyed the brief time with them. Their laughter and obvious joy thrilled me enough.

The fourth and different type of experience took place while I was walking on the campus of the College of San Mateo, contemplating what options I might have regarding my future after leaving Notre Dame de Namur University. Suddenly a small bird descended and remained in flight immediately above my head for several minutes. I didn't hear a voice from heaven as Jesus did at His baptism but did hear the pleasant chirping of the bird, which seemed to convey this message, "Don't worry. I will take care of you. Be strong and trust in me." From that moment I knew my future was secure. God had spoken directly to me.

I can't explain to anyone's satisfaction, even my own, why I so often feel the presence of an ethereal being hovering over or around me. Nor can I understand or provide reasons for the supernatural experiences I have had. I can only conclude that some mysterious but genuine form of communication takes place at times and I enjoy and benefit from the experience.

Chapter 11

>>>))((<<<

My Forgotten Singing Career

As a child, I knew I enjoyed singing and I sometimes dreamed of becoming a professional singer. I had determination, perseverance and plenty of self-discipline but no knowledge of how to enter the music profession or the world in which a singer was expected to function. I long feared my voice would remain in the shower.

Dad had a pleasant voice but no musical training. My half-brother, Jack, boasted a strong tenor voice and early on decided he would pursue the operatic musical route. He studied in Hollywood for several years under the tutelage of a prominent classical singer. He served as chauffeur for the singer for a period of time in order to get free voice lessons.

My fascination with vocal music originated in church and involved primarily the Southern Gospel music tradition as well as honky-tonk and country-Western music. Mother and Dad belonged to the group of Southern migrants forced to California in the 1930s because of the Dust Bowl, and those migrants brought the gospel-country-Western music traditions with them.

Congregations sang Southern Gospel music to express both their personal and group faith regarding Biblical teachings and the Christian life. Groups of four singers, quartets, consisted almost exclusively of talented males who tended to personalize the focus on faith while providing Christian entertainment.

Even though I enjoyed some of the music, the country-Western and Southern Gospel music traditions represented a social class of which I was a part and from which I wanted to escape. I failed to recognize and appreciate not only the professional but also the financial advantages I could have enjoyed as a gospel, country-Western singer. Competence in that type of music might have provided the path of escape to a new life in classical and operatic music.

I began voice lessons at the age of twelve, and my vocal coach, Mark Beck, reflected Hollywood during its Golden Era in the 1930s and 1940s. He had been active in the development of the movies designed for escapism during the Great Depression and viewed himself as an integral part of the American culture and social history of that era.

Mark focused on the Sinatra-Martin type of popular music for which he felt my voice was suited, but he didn't oppose classical pieces for me as long as they didn't require extensive vocal training. He sometimes expressed the opinion that I could quite easily progress to classical music as I matured.

I don't recall too many details about the coach, but I do remember that he drove a Packard, a luxury automobile during its time. The last Packard was manufactured in 1958, and he sported one of the models built in the early 1950s. To him, the Packard symbolized his former wealth and accomplishments before losing his fortune when the Hollywood Golden Era ended.

The accompanist, Josie Lillian, hailed from the opulent spectacle known as the Ziegfeld Follies and still sported the artificially elaborate clothing and demeanor of that era. She cherished her role as one of the young, minor celebrities who had marched up and down flights of stairs dressed as birds or other objects and creatures.

Josie was an excellent accompanist and inspired vocalists to put forth every effort to succeed. Even after I discontinued my vocal lessons with the coach with whom she worked, Josie would accompany me to my various musical gigs. I would pick her up from and return her to her home. She never asked me to pay her. She often said, "I like your voice and enjoy being with you. Your singing has life."

"Thank you," was all I could say.

Josie and I had difficulty communicating verbally. She had emigrated from Europe, had performed in the Follies but had spent little time learning the English language. But her ability to communicate through her music was fantastic. During our practice sessions, she would sometimes change the rhythm of a piece or play the piano more loudly or softly to subtly tell me how she felt I could better interpret the music. She became an important support for me during both practice sessions and performances.

In middle school, I sang regularly on a local radio show sponsored by a small church. Each program featured a short Bible message with three or four gospel solos and duets. I most often served as the soloist but sometimes joined other local singers in performing the duets.

In high school, I accepted a job as a soloist in the local Presbyterian Church. The pastor, Reverend James Bishop, approached me at one of the talent programs in which I participated and asked, "I had heard a great deal about your talent but had not had the pleasure of listening to you until tonight. I now know why you are often dubbed a "song bird" in the press. Would you be willing to work with me as a soloist?"

I was honored and immediately responded, "Yes, it would be an honor." I served as soloist for more than two years.

While still in high school, I was featured on Doye O'Dell's daily kids show called "Cowboy Thrills" and sang at McDonald's Ballroom in Compton, California, where country-vocal luminaries hung out and performed regularly. I recall standing next to and talking with Tex Ritter, Tom Ritter's father, following one performance. I also remember interacting with Bob Wills and His Texas Playboys and Tex Williams.

My supposed "TV Debut" in the Los Angeles area was announced in the local press in 1955, the year after my graduation from high school. The announcement read, in part:

Local friends...can see and hear the bass-baritone make his television debut ... when he will appear on 'Sandy's Hayride,' KTTV, Channel 11.

While serving as church soloist, I began to consider music as a career and entered Pepperdine College at the age of seventeen as a music major. The music curriculum involved piano lessons, voice coaching and music theory, composition and history. The piano instructor, a Southern belle who loved to treat me like a coveted possession, seemed to want me to be comfortable more than she wanted me to succeed on the piano. I enjoyed taking the private lessons she offered but never felt I learned much.

I worked hard in every music class but determined to focus on the further development of my vocal capability. The vocal coaching included private lessons with a prestigious instructor with whom my brother Jack had become acquainted and who was quite well known for his vocal talents.

While working with the private vocal coach, I tentatively decided to specialize in Vocal Performance and develop a distinct vocal style. I was very naïve and found it difficult to determine the style I felt was appropriate for me or with which I would feel comfortable. I continued to toy with classical and opera but eventually decided that my voice was not appropriate for that genre. I couldn't bring myself to accept the fact that country-Western music might be my best choice. I remained conflicted.

I joined the Pepperdine Chorus at the beginning of my second academic year. Most of the music was performed a cappella, and the director, Mr. Brown, had lots of energy and encouraging words for members of the chorus. It was during my first year as a member of the Chorus that Ms. Gloria Gloryn entered my life.

Gloria had a very nice voice and seemed to have a real passion for music. I watched her during each rehearsal but didn't have the courage to approach her. Finally, she sought me out after a choral rehearsal and asked, "Are you willing to sing duets? I enjoy performing but not as a soloist."

I thought for a minute and responded, "Why not? I would love to have a musical partner." We had some two musically productive years together, and during those two years, I never confided to Gloria that my original agreement to sing with her was based both on her musical ability and my personal interest in her. I remember thinking I could spend the rest of my life with her, but she was unfortunately engaged to a military person who had been deployed overseas. She seemed very much in love with him. I never had the courage to tell her how much I admired her personally.

"Refreshing as an ocean breeze on a hot summer day." Gloria and I represented, in part, that breeze intended to provide relaxation during a "community-sing" event in Los Angeles. Our sponsor was the Los Angeles Bureau of Music.

Soon after the "community sing," we presented a sacred concert at a prominent Baptist church and appeared on the television program "Church Talent Hour."

During the two musical years together, Gloria and I entered several vocal contests and won first place. Our financial rewards were not great, but the satisfaction we derived from our performances did motivate us to practice more and more and perform as often as possible.

Our repertoire of songs included light classical, Western and novelty numbers. We interspersed solos and duets for variety and provided our own accompaniment, she on the piano and I on the guitar.

During my second year of partnering with Gloria, I met Mahin, and as soon as she came into my life, everything changed. A possible musical career became totally secondary to my relationship with her.

One evening after we had been dating for several months and Mahin knew I was serious about our relationship, she queried, "Do you really plan to be a professional vocalist? What future does that have for you?"

I really didn't have a response and merely said, "What is your thought?"

"My family would not look favorably on a son-in-law who earns his living as a vocalist. The family members would not be opposed to someone who could sing well but would find a professional singer somewhat anathema to family tradition," she offered.

That brief conversation changed my entire approach to life. I immediately gave up any musical ambitions and purposed to follow Mahin's lead in pursuing my academic career. For years I never even thought about singing. Once in a while a Persian friend would ask me to sing at a small gathering, particularly during the Christmas season, in Tehran. Music became almost persona non grata and vanished from my mind and even vocabulary. Mahin became my preoccupation.

I do not regret having abandoned a career or attempted career in music for almost fifty years of marital bliss, but I do sometimes think it may still not be too late to make a comeback. The major question is: Would the comeback be as a country-Western singer sporting a cowboy hat and boots?

Chapter 12

>>>))(((<<

A World Without Borders:
A Blended Marriage

East was not the east nor west the west; the blended culture without borders that Mahin and I produced for ourselves became increasingly exciting as the years passed. The old world became a part of the new world while the new world blended into the old without excessive stress or strain. We enjoyed some forty-eight years of intercultural bliss before her untimely death in 2006 when she was only seventy-three.

Mahin intrigued me from my first glimpse of her. She was not pretentious. Her dark eyes spoke volumes of wisdom, a combination of self-assurance, humility and compassion. She was slim but not sickly thin. She sported short, raven-black hair and represented a charming combination of the old and new worlds and seemed at home in both. She hadn't bidden farewell to the social sophistication of the Iranian upper class, but she showed a strong willingness to explore the world with an open human heart. Anyone who met her came away with a feeling of elation and friendship. She had, and still has, more friends than I can name.

I'll never forget that unforgettable moment when I first laid eyes on the love of my life.

"Hi," I whispered, sheepishly. "My name is Frank."

"Nice to meet you, Frank," she answered without hesitation. "My name is Mahin."

I couldn't think of anything else to say, not even the fact that I already knew her name. I just stood, admiring her and wishing I had the courage to ask her for a date. Finally, toward the end of the party at a friend's house in Los Angeles which both of us serendipitously attended, I summoned the courage to approach her again.

"I would love to have coffee with you. Are you free next week some time?"

"Yes," she answered. "Just name the night, and we can go to the coffee shop in Westwood Village after I finish my homework."

I left the party, floating on a cloud. I had managed to get a date with a beautiful lady I had met just that evening. That was a first for me.

Our initial date was a little awkward. I didn't know exactly what to talk about, and Mahin seemed reluctant to lead the discussion. But we enjoyed our cup of coffee and made plans for our next rendezvous.

It was on the third date that I discovered I had found my soul mate. We decided that night to go for a hamburger, something that both of us loved at the time. Mahin was living in the women's dormitory at Pepperdine College and was serving as a dormitory counselor. She finished her homework a little later than usual that night, and we didn't leave the college campus until around 9:30 p.m.

From the beginning of that evening, I was worried. I knew the dormitory doors were closed at 11:00 p.m., and I wondered what Mahin would do if we happened to be a little late. As a dormitory counselor she had to set an example for the other residents.

"What if we arrive back after 11:00 p.m.?" I queried. "How will you get into the dorm, and what will the other residents say about you being late?"

"Don't worry," Mahin responded. "Nothing will happen."

We went for our hamburger, got to talking and suddenly realized the time was 11:30 p.m. When I looked at my watch, I was beside myself, but Mahin didn't seem fazed by the lateness of the hour. As we drove back to campus, the conversation was sparse; when we reached the dormitory I asked, "Are you sure you can get into the building without creating a disturbance?"

"Just relax," she answered and walked leisurely toward the window of her dorm room.

When we arrived at the window, I was stupefied. She casually lifted the blinds, wriggled through the window and then leaned out to kiss me good night.

"You worry too much," she said. "Get a good night's rest. I'll see you in a day or two." Then she closed the blinds, leaving me standing outside her window. Fortunately, the guard didn't come around until I was well along the 'Cloud Nine promenade" toward my car.

My infatuation with Mahin soon developed into a strong love. The more I got to know her, the more her character appealed to me, and she appeared to become increasingly fond of me. We continued dating on a regular basis for over a year, not wanting to rush into a legal commitment that would give neither one of us the mutual security we sought. After eighteen months, during one of our several-a-week dates, I popped the question.

"Will you marry me?" I knew Mahin was fond of me but wasn't sure she would agree to marriage.

"Yes," she answered. "But you must realize that I need to finish my degree and have two years left. I may even want to go on to graduate school."

She could have asked for ten years and the opportunity to complete five degrees. If she were willing to be my wife, I was willing to support her, or at least help support her, through as many degrees as she wanted. Her own financial situation provided some of the needed support.

Our wedding ceremony occurred in the Presbyterian Church in Wilmington, California in January 1959. I had for some time served as a soloist at the church, and the pastor readily agreed to perform the ceremony without charge. An acquaintance offered his cabin in Big Bear to us free of charge for some five days. The "freebies" helped us get started. We didn't have much money and whatever funds we had were needed for tuition and other college expenses.

Neither Mahin nor I sought the permission from our families for the marriage. I believe Mahin wrote her family about our decision; she and I visited Mother and Dad to make the announcement to them.

Mahin's family boasted a variety of marriage models: intra-family, inter-family, and cross-cultural. Travel, study abroad and intellectual curiosity had prompted the family to develop beyond the traditional Persian marital inbreeding.

My family was not sufficiently sophisticated to consider potential mates within a particular psychological or social framework. Married three times, Dad never showed signs of giving thought to the type of woman he would marry, nor did he consider the probable level of compatibility between his family and the one into which he was entering. His various unions seemed to be more emotionally than intellectually oriented, nor were they psychologically or socially pondered. Mother, too, always appeared oblivious to the broader considerations of marriage.

The differences between our two families in the approach to marriage were considerable; even though Dad did not understand the differences, he wondered why I couldn't find someone "less different from us." Despite the variation in marriage models existing within Mahin's family, one of her brothers accidentally broke a rib when he began pounding his chest on hearing Mahin was marrying an American.

Our wedding preparation and ceremony completely ignored Persian traditions. There was no lavish engagement party. My parents were living in a mobile home when we became engaged, prohibiting any social events. Mahin's family was too far away to serve as a venue for pre-wedding festivities. No financial matters were discussed or negotiations conducted.

Some six individuals participated in the actual ceremony, which took only a few minutes. Then Mahin and I were off on our limited-budget honeymoon. Traditional Persian wedding ceremonies are large, glorious and well attended. Our simple wedding was small and uneventful, but it launched us on a wonderful, extremely eventful, and definitely unorthodox life journey.

Although I was too naïve to realize it at the time, our marriage soon showed signs of potential difficulties. A number of questions arose, including whether or not her family and/or mine would understand our intercultural relationship and its intricacies. I began asking myself if I were behaving properly to ensure the continuation of the marriage. I didn't want to do things the way my family had always done them, but in situation after situation, I was uncertain as to whether I was meeting Mahin's needs and expectations. Because of my relationship with Mother and Dad, I professed low expectations but actually har-

bored high expectations when it came to personal acceptance, and I thought Mahin might feel the same
way. I would find myself bristling over finances and
even household chores, but Mahin would quietly suggest I back off and cool down before we discussed any
matter related to the home or money. Her quiet demeanor slowly convinced me that her expectation of
me primarily involved a willingness to listen, discuss
and reason and arrive at a reasonable compromise. She
had learned to manage her expectations logically, and
she wanted me to do the same.

My family had never done anything in a particular way or with much thought as to the outcome,
and I had no basis for evaluating my social skills either
within the American or the Iranian community. At
times I was lost, not knowing how to react in certain
situations or when I might embarrass Mahin. For example, in Iran I didn't understand when to stand up if
a lady entered a room, not deducing that I should rise
for the entrance of a friend or acquaintance but not a
servant. Several times I got up when a servant entered
the room, thinking I was showing the proper respect.
Only after several occurrences of such behavior did I
learn the proper protocol.

Whenever I committed a social blunder, Mahin
would engage those around us in conversation. She
was not a jokester, but she would begin a light dialogue
totally foreign to the situation in which I had erred.
She noted my social blunders only when we were

alone, and she thought I might be ready to take and properly process instruction/correction. She was very mature.

The one interest that both of us seemed to have was the motivation and desire to learn about each other's culture; this interest proved all sustaining. Neither of us felt that our culture or family necessarily did everything the right way. I, personally, never deceived myself into thinking that everything had to be done my way. Mahin seemed to have the same approach. This common attitude held us in good stead as we navigated the treacherous waters of newly married life.

Originally, our worldviews were totally at odds, and the ways we dealt with life's challenges clearly showed what at first appeared to be irreconcilable differences. I approached life with a fear of doing wrong and being punished eternally; she had no fear of sinning under a form of religious law or receiving eternal punishment. My behavior stemmed from religious "dos" and "don'ts." A code of uninhibited ethics guided her behavior.

Our judgments and opinions clearly reflected our divergent worldviews. I made decisions out of fear and uncertainty. I, for example, hesitated to take dance lessons even though Mahin was a good dancer and I had always wanted to learn how to dance. She arranged private lessons at the Arthur Murray Studio in downtown Los Angeles. I worked with the instructor for a few weeks but then declared that I didn't really have a sense of rhythm. That declaration was a copout. I feared someone might see me outside the studio and tell someone I knew from the church I was attending that I was dancing in a public place. I also was afraid I might go to "Hell." This fear persisted even though I was in my twenties. I decided to forego the dance lessons.

Mahin based her decisions on potential enjoyment and relaxation.

"I just was not made to be a dancer. I have no sense of rhythm and am clumsy," I told her.

"Are you sure you are telling me the real reasons for not continuing the lessons?" Mahin responded. "I have watched you, and you seem to do quite well. And how could you not have rhythm if you have sung professionally since you were a teenager?"

I had no logical or convincing answer and decided not to respond. Keeping my fears and real reasons for not continuing something I truly enjoyed took precedence over openness and truthfulness even with Mahin.

Mahin's understanding and overall sophistication gradually encouraged me to expose my internal feelings and fears. The longer we remained together the more nearly alike our worldviews became. I gradually escaped from my prison of religious legalism, and Mahin asked me to join her on her journey toward spiritual fulfillment. Each morning both of us would ask ourselves, "What can we do today to make our lives better and increase our spiritual understanding?" We would attempt to discover the answer to the question and do what the answer seemed to suggest. The spiritual became more important than the religious. We could discuss a plethora of topics from a spiritual rather than a religious perspective. Our spiritual connection continues even today, several years after Mahin's passing.

A major advantage both Mahin and I enjoyed from the outset of our marriage was our openness to new ideas and our reluctance to dismiss suggestions and opinions out of hand. We, Mahin at times more than I, were willing to meet challenges and deal with them as partners. Our forced departure from Iran after the Islamic Revolution and our struggle to reestablish ourselves here in the United States even strengthened our partnership. I wasn't always the leader of the team, but when I served as a follower, I knew I had an outstanding leader who had my best interest at heart. After some time together, complete trust characterized our marriage.

Mahin and I were open with each other but not with others. Keeping things to ourselves that might shock or hurt someone else seemed to be a part of both of our psychological natures. From the outset, Mahin was much more sociable than I, but from her I learned enough to enjoy people and interact with them without being judgmental.

Around-the-world vacations together were always a blessing and much fun. Shortly after we were married, and while we were both in university, we went to Tijuana, Mexico to attend the bullfights and jai alai games. We enjoyed the excitement among the spectators and sometimes got caught up in the ferocity of the contest between the bull and the matador.

Mahin loved to gamble and would sometimes drag me to Las Vegas. She was not the type to bet our lives away, but she did enjoy and successfully played several card games. I never understood cards and could only play the slot machines, but after three or four years I came to enjoy watching her play and/or dropping coins into the machine, waiting for her to finish a game.

Our first international trip together took place in 1964, the year Mahin received her Master of Science degree in Public Health and I was awarded my Doctorate of Education degree in Middle East Studies and Comparative Education. We graduated in June and left almost immediately for Iran via Europe. Mahin decided we would travel across the Atlantic Ocean by ship and made all the arrangements. We boarded the ship in New York after attending the 1964 World's Fair. Mahin's sister Esmat accompanied us.

I had never been on a ship before and had not traveled outside the United States except to Canada in the late 1950s. Initially, I enjoyed the party atmosphere on the ship but the realization we were on the ocean with no land in sight frightened me. Mahin assuaged my fears and finally calmed me down. By the time we landed in England, I had adjusted pretty well to the ship and the water.

Europe itself presented another situation. In England, I had considerable difficulty understanding the policemen and particularly those individuals who spoke with a cockney accent. I remember that once I had to ask Mahin to translate for me. I had requested directions from a policeman, but no matter how hard I tried, I could not grasp what he was telling me. Mahin seemed to have little, if any, difficulty in understanding the "bobby." She quickly told me what he was saying, and we moved on toward our desired destination.

On the same trip, we had more than the usual number of suitcases. After all, we were going to Iran for one or two years. Incidentally, we remained in Iran for fifteen years and would have stayed longer if the Islamic Revolution had not occurred. The suitcases burdened our trip from the airport into Venice, Italy. We traveled by water taxi and an attempt to get all the valises into the taxi proved to be a monumental task. That particular trip taught me to travel light.

The night we arrived in Tehran I felt I had come home. The family greeted me at the airport as if I had long been one of them. The following weeks were filled with parties and visitations to and from members of the extended family. I soon developed a bad case of diarrhea, which persisted for six plus months, but the possibility of realizing my childhood dreams of visiting Daniel's tomb, the city of Susa and other historical sites kept me motivated and determined to get well.

I recall attending a cockfight on the island of Bali in Indonesia with Mahin. The driver we hired for several days suggested we witness a fight and we reluctantly agreed to do so. Neither Mahin nor I had ever seen such a brutal display of competition and were somewhat put off by it. The razor blades bound to the feet of the roosters would wound or kill opponents. Blood would flow freely with no signs of remorse from the cock owners or competition organizers. The fatally injured roosters would flop around on the ground and the healthy cocks attempt to attack their wounded mates if allowed to do so. The scene was a wild mixture of blood and cock's combs. We, however, didn't leave the arena prior to the conclusion of the various rounds of competition and certainly had something to talk about over dinner.

One U.S. Chamber of Commerce trip to Asia took us not only to Hong Kong and what was then known as The Territories but also to Singapore where we were the guests of the U.S. ambassador for a lovely party at the embassy. We enjoyed first-class hotels and outstanding meals.

Another year we visited Spain, Monaco and Denmark. From Europe, I proceeded to Saudi Arabia where I accepted a position with the Ford Foundation and later UNESCO. For more than a year, I flew regularly from Saudi to Lebanon, Iran and other parts of the Middle East to carry out my professional duties.

With our younger daughter Rana, we went to parts of Italy and attended the Mozart Festival in Salzburg, Austria. This particular trip was strictly for pleasure and was intended to introduce our daughter to Europe.

All in all, our travels were both educational and very enjoyable. I don't think that either one of us ever tired of going to countries with cultures different from our own or learning about ideas and practices that were somewhat foreign to both of us. The travel, I believe, greatly enriched our marriage and helped us form a cultural bond based on our common experiences and our determination to develop a global perspective unimpeded by nationalistic or ethnic biases.

I believe our intercultural marriage was highly successful and became a sustaining force for both Mahin and me. It certainly proved to be a stabilizer for the development of my social as well as intellectual skills. Why was our marriage so successful and enjoyable? We loved each other as well as each other's culture and language. We incorporated the values of each culture into our common culture. We not only adapted, but also changed and remained accountable to each other. We learned to negotiate our differences and benefitted from our negotiations. In short, we became partners with a common goal: to understand each other, succeed in life and cherish our time together.

Every marriage experiences disappointments, obstacles and some rough times; ours was no exception. In a very short period of time after the Islamic Revolution, we lost approximately one million dollars of our savings, and we had to start over when we returned to the United States after fifteen years of residency in Iran. Neither Mahin nor I could find a job after our return for almost five years. We were, of course, worried and sometimes frightened, but we never gave up.

I believe the success of our marriage and its longevity resulted from growing up together, having patience with each other and those around us, maintaining open minds to our ethnic, religious and socio-economic differences and simply loving each other more each day.

Chapter 13

>>>>>>))((((<<

My Extended Family:
Kinship and Dysfunction

Extended families can evoke pleasant mental photographs or anxiety, and my family, unfortunately, most often encouraged the latter. The family was, and still is, relatively narrow in scope but quite dysfunctional, particularly on Dad's side. Mother's side seemed less prone toward dysfunction.

Dad had two ex-wives, who themselves had exhusbands. He had one child by each of his "exes" and two by Mother. The older of the two by Mother passed away at birth.

I know very little about my paternal grandfather. I barely recall that his given name was Charles. He moved in the early years of World War II to Bremerton, Washington, where for several years he labored in the shipyard.

He and Grandma Dickson produced three boys but divorced early on. He remarried and had several children with his second wife.

Only once do I remember accompanying Dad and Uncle Henry, Dad's younger brother, to Bremerton to visit with Grandfather Burroughs. I was around fifteen at the time of the visit, and it was during that visit that my grandfather let me know in no uncertain terms that he didn't care for me. When I entered the house, he proclaimed in a loud voice: "The little professor has come. Watch how you talk."

I still do not know whether the comment was meant only for my ears, but it certainly had a chilling effect on me. I wanted to leave the house immediately but didn't because of Dad and Uncle Henry.

Grandfather Burroughs hardly said anything to me throughout our visit. He wouldn't even look at me, choosing to ignore me rather than engage me in even the simplest conversation. Based on that experience, I chose never to see him again.

Grandma Dickson had one sister whom I referred to as Aunt Florence. Her married name was Lynn, but she had been widowed before my birth and, to my knowledge, had never remarried. She had four children, two daughters and two sons. One of the sons suffered from a rather severe disability caused by an auto accident. The other son I hardly recall. I know the older daughter, Evy, was married and had one son. I don't remember much about the second daughter, Amy. I rarely saw most of Aunt Florence's children and eventually lost touch with them.

Grandma Dickson's aunt, whose name I can't recall, lived in Sacramento, California. She would visit Grandma once or twice each year, and I enjoyed her company very much. She always wanted to have fun, played the harmonica and loved to tell jokes. She must have been in her eighties when I saw her, but she always seemed sharp and very happy. Nothing about her background or family was ever discussed.

My half-sister, Inez, the product of Dad's second marriage, displayed characteristics similar to those of Queen Elizabeth I in relation to the male gender. She had several boyfriends, but unlike the queen, she also had three husbands.

I heard Inez chose her men primarily for their sexual prowess, ignoring their looks and wisdom. Indiscretion characterized her relationships with several of them.

Her first marriage was to a war veteran who appeared to have psychological problems. Perhaps the difficulties developed during or after the military experience, but at the time little was known or said about psychological problems experienced by military personnel after combat. It was assumed that such problems were personal in nature and should be handled discreetly.

Two or three times I accompanied Dad to Broken Bow, Oklahoma and Texarkana, Texas, where Inez and her husband lived for brief periods of time. Dad was responding to urgent calls from Inez. One call concerned the husband's attempt to commit suicide. He did not succeed in that particular attempt, but I have no idea how his life ended.

The second husband drove a huge Bekins van across country. For a while, he and Inez rented an apartment in Wilmington not far from where Mother and Dad and Grandma Dickson lived. Like their marriage, their residency in Wilmington didn't last long.

Inez had two children: one boy and one girl. Both are probably still living but their whereabouts are unknown to me. The last time I saw her daughter was when we gathered in Hot Springs, Arkansas following Dad's death back in the mid-1970s. I visited with the son briefly in the early-1990s when Mother passed on, but I have not been successful in locating him since then.

For years, I had no news of Inez or her whereabouts; only twice after Mahin and I got married did we reconnect. The first contact was talking with her once by telephone from Washington, D.C. when I applied for a clearance to operate for some two years as a visiting scientist at the U.S. Department of Energy. The second occurred when Mahin, our daughters and I were on our way down Highway 101 from Santa Rosa to Los Angeles. At the time, Inez was living not far from Santa Barbara, and we called ahead and met her at a Denny's Restaurant for about forty-five minutes so she and the girls could see each other. After that meeting, I lost touch and have no clue what finally happened to her. My efforts to reach her by telephone during the last few years have proved futile.

Inez, an attractive but very unfortunate woman, could not seem to settle down with a husband or a male companion. She used her attractiveness to her own detriment. Her stormy marriages were relatively short-term.

My maternal grandmother passed away several years before I was born. She was on her way with her husband, Granddad Robbins, from Arkansas to California as part of the Steinbeck wave of impoverished immigrants in the 1930s when she succumbed to an illness in Mesa, Arizona. Health issues plagued her for several years and her illness prevented her from raising Mother, who was brought up by her grandfather. I'm told I could find Grandmother Robbins' grave somewhere in the Mesa area.

I had three first cousins: two paternal, one maternal. The paternal cousin with whom I have interacted for many years is Helen Burroughs. Her dad seemed to understand children's needs and desires. I visited Helen and her parents only a few times while growing up, but each time I went to their home for a two-or-three-day stay, I enjoyed myself very much.

Helen's mother, was a very attractive woman. Her beauty and mode of dress led to considerable gossip and caused ill feelings between her and the other family members. Later in her life when Mahin and I visited Helen in Virginia, I enjoyed Aunt Winnie's company and found her to be a caring and loving individual.

I didn't get to know Uncle Henry, whom I mentioned earlier regarding my paternal grandfather until a year or so before his death. I always thought he didn't like me and wondered why. One night during one of our visits to Los Angeles in the early 1980s, however, Mahin, Uncle Henry, Aunt Winnie and I went out to dinner. During the dinner, Uncle Henry casually said, "I have always wanted to have a drink with you, and tonight I have been able to do so." How surprised and pleased I was to hear that comment. Uncle Henry's apparent forthrightness helped me overcome the doubt I had long held about his love for me and certainly cinched my love for him. The comment awakened me to the need to understand people for who they are as soon as possible. How many years I had wasted thinking there was no feeling for me on his part! But I am thankful I learned of his affection for me prior to his death.

Helen and I seemed to have little in common when we were children, but now I realize that Dad contributed to our psychological estrangement. While Mother, Dad and I lived in Arkansas, she and Grandma Dickson came to visit us one summer. The summer heat encouraged us to take off our shoes and run about very often on an unpaved street. Helen wasn't used to running around without shoes.

I was, at least I thought, a hard-core Arkansan. I could walk, even run, barefooted over pebbles and rocks without hurt or pain, and I simply could not understand why Helen couldn't do the same. Both of us were only about six years old; my logic and empathy had not developed to any great extent. I now know

Helen's feet simply were not used to rocks and unpaved surfaces and weren't as tough as mine; the soles
of my feet had become calloused from going without
shoes, particularly during the hot summer months.

My appreciation for Helen grew when she spent
some time with us in Iran in 1968. She stayed with us
for only a few weeks but remained in Iran for almost a
year. At the time, the Government of Iran readily
granted visas to Americans. Her skills were much
needed and welcomed by the U.S. companies. I think
it was during her stay in Tehran that I enticed her to
smoke a cigarette, which she apparently had not done
for several years. Fortunately, she didn't take up the
habit again, and I abandoned it not too many years later.

In the mid-1970s, I became the Executive Director of the United States Chamber of Commerce in
Tehran. Earlier, Helen had joined the White House
staff under President Richard Nixon but later transferred to the U.S. Department of Commerce, under
whose auspices she would sometimes travel to Iran as
the advance person for the Secretary of Commerce.
My position in the Chamber sometimes required me to
visit Washington, D.C. It was during these visits that
Helen and I became better acquainted and developed a
mutual appreciation. The bond between us now ena-
bles us to travel together comfortably and thoroughly
enjoy each other's company. For me, she substitutes

for the sister I really never got to know. She is a confi-
dante I can't imagine being without.

Helen's brother, the second paternal cousin, and
I never got to know each other. He was somewhat
younger than Helen and I; I hardly spent any time with
him. He passed away at an early age. I have only vague
memories of him, and most of those were after he had
become an adult.

I spent enjoyable summers with my only maternal first cousin, Don Robbins, in Hot Springs, Arkansas. Mother, Dad and I had moved back to California by the time I was in middle school, and the time
I spent in Arkansas after returning to California was
during the summer. When I was in high school, Mother and I would drive to Hot Springs once school was
out in California and remain there for four to six
weeks.

The days were long and relaxing. The mornings
sometimes involved lessons in the game of bridge or
just lolling around. Seldom were there other young
people with us other than our girl friends and my
friend's mother, who was teaching the four of us the
game of bridge. The girl whom I dated was Don's
cousin on his mother's side.

Sometimes Don and I would go down to the
lake or visit a fast-food restaurant, a place where one
could get curb service. Even in the evening we might
drive our girl friends to such a place for a hamburger
and fries, our favorite food at the time.

The first federally-protected area in the United States, Hot Springs, had long been a gambling center and was known for its lively lifestyle, but its luster as a gaming town had begun to fade. Many of the gambling operatives and associated groups had moved elsewhere; those remaining were considering moves to other areas. Today, the downtown that once was alive with all types of activities appears calm, almost eerily quiet. At least that was the case the last time I visited Hot Springs.

The thermal baths were famous and extremely relaxing. Each time I passed the beautiful bathhouse row, I remembered that one of Dad's distant cousins had for many years served as a masseur in one of the bathhouses. As a child growing up in Hot Springs, Dad took me to the bathhouse to visit our cousin.

As with the gambling establishments, the bathhouses slowly ceased operations by the time we spent our summers in the area. The beautiful bathhouse row with its magnificent magnolia trees began to resemble the rest of Hot Springs: beautifully constructed vintage buildings with no activity and severe deterioration. The bathhouses were owned and originally operated by the U.S. Government, but the government seemed to have forgotten about them. Gradually, attempts were made to lease the various buildings to private operators.

From childhood I had been fond of Hot Springs. It was a friendly, historic town many visitors seemed to fall in love with. The hospitality of the residents seemed superb. The town boasted of fascinating stories of mafia-like characters and the skullduggery that supposedly accompanied the gambling. The accounts of the horse races that occurred from spring through fall intrigued me.

As a child I became enthralled with the many crystals available in the roadside stands along the highways near Hot Springs. I thought they were beautiful stones when converted into rings. At the time, I was not aware of the charm the crystals held for individuals involved in esoteric healing practices, nor did I know that Indian tribes had long believed them to be sacred. Hot Springs quartz crystals continue to intrigue tourists even today.

Geologists consider the quartz crystals found around Hot Springs to be of the highest quality. They come in several shapes, including clusters and points. They boast a variety of colors, from clear to dark blue. Jewelers convert them into very attractive jewelry. At one time, individuals were able to hunt for their own beautiful crystals from a number of mines relatively inexpensively.

To me, adventure lived in Hot Springs, and I thought it was the perfect place for a combination of relaxing activities and let-your-hair-down vacations.

During the summers, church on Sunday was a necessity. Sometimes my cousin Don and I were also expected to attend the mid-week services at the Baptist church in Magnet Cove, a village near Hot Springs, where Don's father, Uncle Lawrence, served as pastor. I didn't have to attend a Pentecostal church if Dad wasn't with us.

Because of his work and church-related responsibilities, Dad didn't spend summers in Arkansas with Mother and me. During these vacation periods, I seldom spent time reading books. I studied hard during the academic year and wanted to do something besides studying during the month spent in Hot Springs. Don was more an athlete than a bookworm.

Neither Don nor I liked hanging around the house all day and spent much of our time cruising around town in Don's car. We had no siblings and could enjoy each other's company without interruption or interference from family competitors.

A sense of urgency usually developed in the final two weeks of our stay in Hot Springs. I was determined to have fun and enjoy not only Don but his delightful teenage cousin also, one of the few girls I could comfortably date. I knew I wouldn't see her again until the next summer. Since she was family, I didn't have to worry about what she thought of me. I realized that the carefree days and feelings of complete freedom were rapidly coming to an end and I would have to return to California and a busy year at college. I didn't even look forward to shopping for clothes for the academic year or following a particular routine. Each relaxed summer spoiled me, but I knew

I had to complete my degree if I wanted to have a successful career in a profession yet undetermined.

During the academic year, I spent so much time on the college campus that professors and fellow students often became my temporary extended family. The fleetingness of the relationships didn't, however, allow me to become really involved with them.

The summers in Hot Springs with Don enabled me to be with part of my extended family in a non-threatening setting that let me relax and be myself. It seemed that our minds came in contact with each other more in the month or six weeks we spent together during the summer than those of most other members of my extended family in California. Together we could hammer out principles and rules of social engagement that were appropriate for me throughout the rest of the year on the anvil of temporary, everyday association.

My half-brother, Jack, was more than fifteen years older than I. Had he been a little younger, he might have been a friend "provided by nature," but the age difference and his periods of absence from my life didn't allow closeness.

Some research has indicated that an age gap of more than four years is probably not optimal for mental stimulation between siblings; the huge age gap between Jack and me prevented or at least discouraged any type of companionship or affection between us until later in life. Jack hardly knew my personality. He was a potential friend, but an actual friendship between us didn't develop until both of us were well into adulthood.

The relationship between Jack and me and between our families actually evolved after our forced return to the United States from Iran following the Islamic Revolution. I was so confused and depressed on reentering the U.S. that I couldn't readily make a logical decision. I probably should have gone directly to Washington, D.C. where I still had some contacts from my time with the U.S. Chamber of Commerce in Tehran, but I thought Jack might be able to help me get a teaching job at a college in Sonoma County or nearby. He had tenure at Santa Rosa Junior College, and I was sure he could pull some strings to get me started on a new career. But shortly after our return to the U.S., Jack left his job at the junior college on disability and had relatively little to do with the college after his departure.

He and his wife Kay were, however, very good to us. They allowed the four of us—Mahin, our two daughters, Ladan and Rana, and me—to stay in their home until we could find a place to live, get the girls in school and furnish the condominium we bought after about three months. The condominium was within a few miles of Jack and Kay's residence and this close proximity permitted me to get acquainted with Jack for the first time and to realize how generous he and Kay could be. Jack is now deceased, but I still enjoy being in touch with Kay, a wonderful person who continues to serve as my connection to a brother I had grown fond of later in life.

My uncles and aunts on both sides of my family were a mixture of functionality and "dysfunctionality." Uncle Garland, Mother's brother, passed away recently at 101 years of age. He had an interesting life, living until he was in his eighties in Bishop, California, roaming the surrounding mountains, staking claims for mines when he discovered gold or other metals. He continued his prospecting until he fell down a mountain and decided he should take up other hobbies. He then moved to Hot Springs, later to Miami, Florida and still later to Tennessee where he died of a heart attack.

Another of Mother's brothers died quite early from heavy drinking. The third brother died from lung cancer brought on by heavy smoking. The latter brother was cousin Don's father and the pastor of the small Baptist church in Magnet Cove, Arkansas, where cousin Don and I attended Sunday service and sometimes Wednesday-night prayer meeting during my summer sojourns in Arkansas.

On Dad's side of the family, one brother drank heavily and died relatively young. The other brother, Uncle Henry, Helen's dad, lived an apparently rewarding life and died peacefully in his seventies.

I was particularly close to Aunt Edna, my aunt by marriage on Mother's side. She served as the pastor's wife and sometimes took care of me when we lived in Arkansas. She encouraged me very much when I was a child and had considerable influence on my personal development.

My extended family has been quite dysfunctional through the years, but certain members of the family have been and continue to be precious to me. The kinship has helped me overcome any wariness about family connections. No matter how dysfunctional, the family members are part of me and I am a part of them. I imagine that dysfunction typically exists in families and I'm comforted by that fact.

Chapter 14

>>>>)))((((<<<<

The Family in Tehran:
A New Culture and Learning Experience

"We are approaching Mehrabad Airport. Please have your documents ready to show the Iranian authorities."

Although anticipated, the airline steward's announcement threw me into a state of both shock and anticipation. I could hardly believe I was actually entering the country that housed so many of the sites, history and stories of ancient personalities that had intrigued me since childhood: the famous Achaemenid king, Cyrus the Great, who had shown extreme kindness to the Jews; Queen Esther, who replaced Vashti as queen of the Achaemenid Empire and the bravery she had shown in asking for help for the Jews; and, Daniel in the lion's den. Aside from Iran's rich history, my anticipation focused on my new family.

After brief pleasantries at the airport, Mahin, her sister Esmat and I were off to the home where we would live for the next year. Located in central Tehran, the house was on a narrow street referred to as a *koocheh*. While it didn't boast the elegance of the mansions in North Tehran, it reflected the vernacular or more traditional Persian residential architecture, which included elements from both Islamic and pre-Islamic eras.

The design of the home carefully followed the inward-seeking style common to the traditional Persian residence. It boasted an enclosed patio/courtyard surrounded by high walls of adobe and brick. The windows looked out onto the courtyard, preventing a visual intrusion from the outside world and offering nearly complete privacy.

The floor plan included six rooms on three levels. The basement housed the kitchen and a family dining room. The ground level incorporated primarily the living room where guests were received and entertained and a traditional "squat toilet." The bedrooms comprised the third floor. The furniture had no distinguishing characteristics, but beautiful Persian carpets graced the living room and guest dining area.

A well-maintained "hose" or small pool offered the water needed to wash vegetables and even clothes. Large potted plants added to the garden-like ambiance of the courtyard. The walls and courtyard provided a microcosm of safety and peace from outside tension and disturbances.

From the street the visitor or occupant would enter a transitional space resembling a hallway. From the hallway, one could conveniently access most parts of the house.

The building didn't have central heating, just old-fashioned oil heaters. One of them was installed in the bedroom Mahin and I occupied. I wasn't sure of the need for such a heater, as the weather was still warm when we arrived, but as winter approached, the need for a heater became quite apparent. I often sat directly in front of the heater for long periods of time reading or talking with a newfound Iranian friend who had been trained in Boston but had returned to Iran shortly after our arrival.

During the first week following our arrival, we welcomed a constant stream of visitors, both members of the family and friends. It was amazing to me how many individuals wanted to welcome Mahin and Esmat home and catch a glimpse of the new *damad-e-farangi* (foreign son-in-law). I participated in the conversations and dinners as best I could, but I had only a nodding, academic acquaintance with the Persian culture and language and wanted to avoid as many *faux pas* as possible. I put myself under considerable pressure in an effort to present a proper demeanor.

Soon after our arrival, one of Mahin's brothers, Nematollah, known as Nemat, expressed concern about the length of my brown hair and the counterculture implications for the Iranians I'd be associating with. Mahin and I attended university and graduate school during the cultural phenomena known as the Beat Generation of the 1950s and the Hippie counterculture of the early 1960s; both phenomena attracted me. I didn't become a bohemian hedonist who extolled complete non-conformity and impulsive creativity, nor did I experiment with drugs. I did, however, evolve a strong interest in metaphysics and Eastern religious philosophies and grew my hair fairly long at the time. In my opinion, the slightly-above-shoulder length and the style of my hair clearly showed I was "hip" and fully conscious of social developments.

The longer hair also attested to the California look of the 1960s and Beatle mania. My background in music and show business encouraged me readily to identify with the group; part of the identification involved longer hair.

One day a few weeks after we arrived in Tehran, I attempted to explain the reason for my hair length to Nemat.

"I have entertained professionally for several years," I said. "Audiences in America expect an entertainer's hair to be a little longer than that of the average person."

Nemat listened to the translation of my comment and responded in Persian.

"You're no longer in America," he said. "Here only shorter hair is acceptable. What kind of reputation will you force on Mahin with your extended locks? People will wonder why she married you."

For several weeks, I attempted to rebuff Nemat's complaints about my hairstyle. I couldn't understand why he remained adamant that I sport a shorter style. But gradually I acquiesced to his pleadings and accompanied him to a local barbershop. The shop itself was of the 1940s American vintage with barber chairs that I hadn't seen in Los Angeles for many years. The clippers the barber used were not electric but hand-operated.

I could in no way explain how I wanted my hair cut. I didn't want it too short, just short enough to please Nemat. After several attempts, the barber and I seemed to understand each other and he got to work. The result was not exactly to my liking, but I didn't complain. Nemat paid the barber, walked me back home and immediately exclaimed to Mahin in Persian, "He looks a lot better. I hope he will keep his hair this length. It will be more acceptable to Iranians." Mahin didn't translate the statement for me until several weeks later.

Nemat was one of four brothers. The other three were Ezzatollah, Rahim and Ali. Each brother had a unique personality, had attended university and entered a different professional field. Ezzatollah studied engineering and co-owned a very successful engineering firm, which built many of Iran's roads and CIA's listening posts focused on the Soviet Union. Nemat had studied economics and, at least in theory, worked for the Iranian Ministry of Finance, but he spent little time in the office. Rahim earned a degree in law and also worked for the government. Ali became a teacher and was a closet scholar—he didn't show his scholarly tendencies until you got to know him well.

Nemat hardly had any hair, and the other brothers kept their hair quite short. Neither the Beatles nor the Beat Generation had influenced the generation of Iranians of which the brothers were members.

Following the Islamic Revolution, I was fortunate to be protected in Rahim's residence from the time I fled my office until I departed Iran some ten to twelve days later. Rahim and his wife Farideh hosted a birthday party, which allowed me to see many friends and bid them *adieu*.

I found wisdom in each of the brothers, a willingness to consider various points of view and a spirit of compromise that endeared them to me despite Nemat's insistence that I wear my hair shorter. In my opinion, three of the brothers had one primary vice—a strong penchant for gambling.

I regularly partied with the brothers and their families who visited our home at least once every two weeks. If I needed an official document from the Ministry of Finance, Nemat could be relied on. Rehim cooperated with me as a long-time member of the Ministry of Justice in my attempt to free several Americans from Evin Prison. While we were working on the release, a mob attacked the prison and freed them. Each brother's death saddened me greatly.

Mahin's two sisters, Akram and Esmat, were very different in personality. I never really felt I got to know Akram. When we arrived in Iran, she and her husband were living in Tabriz, northern Iran. After a few years, she and her husband divorced, and she moved back to Tehran and established a small boutique known as the White Peacock. She operated the boutique until she developed a severe heart ailment in the mid-1970s. She opted for surgery in Pittsburgh, Pennsylvania; following the surgery, she didn't return to Iran but came to California, obtained her permanent residency and later her citizenship. She passed on in 2003, only three years before Mahin's passing. Until her death, she remained a sister-in-law with whom I could interact formally but not as an intimate family member.

When I heard Esmat was coming to Los Angeles to live with us for a while not long after Mahin and I were married, I became worried. I thought we didn't share similar life experiences, nor had we gone through comparable life trials. We had spent no time together. Forming a close bond with Esmat as a sister-in-law, I assumed, would be quite difficult. I felt most uneasy about the obvious differences in religious beliefs.

In an effort to avoid undue conflict and misunderstanding, I attempted to become well acquainted with Esmat. I reached beyond my level of comfort to get to know her and hoped she was willing to do the same. I aimed to spend time with her and learn what made her unique. I promised myself I would honor her Persian traditions to the extent I could.

I became acquainted with and developed an appreciation for Esmat's idiosyncrasies in 1960 when

Mahin returned to Iran for several months and left the two of us to share an apartment in downtown Los Angeles.

Mahin took the trip to Tehran to visit the family after several years, and neither Mahin nor I thought about the need for a permanent visa before she left. After all, she was still a student. But after being with the family for several weeks, Mahin introduced herself to the U.S. Embassy in Tehran and informed them she wanted to return to the United States. When embassy personnel discovered she was married to an American, they told her that she could not re-enter the U.S. without a permanent visa and that she needed to obtain the visa prior to leaving Iran. The process took some six months, but persistence paid off. She was granted the visa and returned to the U.S. as a permanent resident.

During Mahin's absence, I was extremely nervous and feared Mahin would not be able to return to the U.S. because we hadn't informed the U.S. Immigration Service of our marriage and her student status. Esmat was in the U.S. on a visitor visa and feared she might have to leave the country before Mahin's return. Together, we fretted every night about the visa situation and commiserated about what might happen. Enjoying ourselves was practically impossible, even if we had a drink or two. I don't think either one of us slept soundly at night until Mahin was back with us in Los Angeles.

Mahin's absence, however, enabled Esmat and me to become well acquainted and somewhat adjusted to each other. Getting acquainted helped keep us in the loop regarding family goings-on in both my family and hers. Esmat continued to share an apartment with us until we left for Iran in 1964.

While Mahin and I worked toward our under-graduate and graduate degrees at Pepperdine and U.C.L.A., Esmat worked at a local hospital, graduated from modeling school and achieved certification as a beautician or hairstylist, a vocation she pursued for a brief period in West Los Angeles in 1963 where she was very popular among the clientele.

During our time in Iran, Mahin and I enjoyed Esmat's casual company and interaction with her at frequent social gatherings. While building our home, we occupied a house Esmat owned in Shemiran on Golestan One Street near the elementary school known as Golestan Koudak, which Ladan and Rana attended until the Islamic Revolution.

Besides Mahin, Esmat was my "caregiver" dur-ing the early years of marriage. She patiently taught me how to interact with a variety of people, helped bring me out of my virtual Pepper Tree Kingdom and guid-ed me through the complicated but beautiful Persian culture.

I benefitted considerably from Esmat's personal and professional introductions in Iran. My association and employment with the Imperial Organization for

Social Services and ultimately the Fifth Asian Games and the 2500th Celebration of the Iranian Monarchy came about as a result of her efforts on my behalf. My work in the latter celebration earned me a *Neshan-e-Homayoun* (Imperial Certificate) signed by His Majesty Mohammad Reza Pahlavi.

Esmat has always been an attractive woman. She never had to worry about gaining weight. Her face was well shaped, and her hair was always in place. She usually dressed fashionably and sported well-manicured nails. Unfortunately, she too often expected other women to match her beauty and could become critical of those who failed to do so.

Over the years, she entertained many suitors, both American and Iranian. Some of the prospects were quite wealthy and prominent. She, however, has never found a soul mate and today remains unmarried at the ripe age of ninety plus, an age at which she requires constant care and attention. It is very difficult for her to accept her need for twenty-four-hour assistance.

Mahin served as Esmat's caregiver until 2006 when she passed, and I assumed the responsibility after Mahin left us. I had never taken care of an elderly person before and I have found caring for Esmat a real challenge. She seems resistant to care and yet simultaneously demanding. She changes her mind very often so no matter what I do, I become the villain. I find it almost impossible to please her or lift her spirits. I am slowly learning how to foster cooperation and avoid or minimize the depression that I experienced when I began the task. I am still determined to avoid the depression and chronic diseases often associated with caregivers.

Despite the difficulties inherent in aging and caretaking, there exists closeness between Esmat and me that can be found between few brothers-in-law and sisters-in-law. We argue and complain about each other but strongly defend each other at the least provocation. She is a true sister to me, and I believe I am a brother to her.

One huge problem from which Esmat has suffered from the time I met her is her tendency toward negativity. Seldom does she find any development positive; she tends to become the victim in most situations. With age, the problem has worsened.

Mahin's mother, *Khanim Jan*, a designation of endearment, which means "dear lady," was a very special person to me. Within a short period of time after our arrival in Iran, I had come to accept her as my own mother. She was engaging, smart and always ready to explain Iranian culture, literature and protocol to me; she would answer my questions on any topic without asking the reason for my inquiry. She and I often had lunch together and enjoyed being together.

Khanim Jan came from a very distinguished background. Her father was one of the leading religious leaders during the 1906 Constitutional Revolution and the very first practicing religious figure to be elected to the Iranian parliament after the adoption of the Iranian Constitution. He received religious training in one of the traditional Shiite schools in Iraq, but throughout his career he promoted the separation of mosque and state. He was a prolific writer but later in life became ill and went to Europe for treatment. He died there and is buried in Berlin.

Khanim Jan grew up at a time in Iran when young women were not encouraged, perhaps even forbidden, to attend school, but she benefitted from a remarkably forward-thinking father and family. Her father provided tutors in a number of subjects and she learned well. She was very conversant in Persian literature, the Qur'an, philosophy and a number of other subjects. I enjoyed listening to her explain a poem or a philosophical concept.

One day at lunch, I picked her brain.

"Can you explain why Rumi was always searching for his 'self'?" I asked.

Khanim Jan thought for a minute and responded, in Persian.

"Rumi searched for his lost teacher for many years," she explained. "But the search allowed him to eventually find himself. I'm not certain he knew he was searching for his self, but his emphasis on finding the teacher encouraged him to be less selfish and more open to Islamic mysticism. The teacher's disappearance, at least in part, lead to Rumi's transformative spiritual experience, and the search resulted in a revelation that he could be his own spiritual universe."

One incident that she shared made quite an impression on me; it occurred early in the reign of Reza Shah Pahlavi. Having been impressed by the modernization of Turkey under Ataturk, Reza Shah visited Turkey and determined to modernize Iran. One of the simple tenets of modernization was the abolition of the *chador*, the covering many Moslem women wear to show their allegiance to Islam. One day *Kahnim Jan* was walking in Tehran in her *chador* and suddenly felt someone pulling on the cloth. She attempted to keep the *chador* around her but soon realized that government agents were working to remove the cloth that supposedly separated her from other women and certainly men on the street. She didn't oppose the government agents. She was totally comfortable in the *chador* or without it. She would laugh when relating the incident and would add a bit of humor that only she could produce. Her demonstrated ability to adapt and remain positive proved inspirational to me.

Authors sometimes refer to the current generation of Iranian women as the "feminist generation" and laud the progress the women have made in liberating themselves despite the strictness and somewhat backward approach to women's affairs displayed by the Government of the Islamic Republic. In one study conducted by Charles Kurzman, a number of female college students and graduates expressed a reluctance to marry because they felt Iranian men and families would not encourage them to pursue their professional ambitions and/or dreams. While I understand the concerns, I easily recall *Khanim Jan* and her intellectual advancement despite the restrictions placed on women during her time and think that with the necessary intellectual curiosity the women could advance themselves despite the societal restrictions. *Khanim Jan* didn't have a college education but enjoyed an outstanding level of intellectual development. Her death in the mid-1970s deeply saddened me.

Khanim Jan had a brother whom most people called *Agha Dai*, "Sir Uncle." This beloved uncle had been trained in Najaf, Iraq, to serve as a religious leader but decided not to serve in that capacity following the completion of his formal training. Instead, he focused on real estate and a career as a member of the Iranian parliament. He was successful at both and was beloved.

I recall visiting with *Agha Dai* numerous times both at his home near the bazaar in Tehran and at his garden in Shemiran and never tired of discussing politics and religion with him. He was open-minded, extremely intelligent and eager to search for the truth rather than declaring that he had the ultimate answer. He knew Middle East politics as no one else I have met. I had the pleasure of being at his bedside when he gained consciousness for the last time before he passed on quietly into his next stage of existence. During his last moment of consciousness, he raised his hand and bid me goodbye. I miss *Agha Dai* very much and often wish I could once again engage in the intense but extremely friendly conversations we had on a variety of topics.

Agha Dai's son, Dr. Mohammad A. Molavi, distinguished himself as one of the first Iranian Ambassadors to the European Common Market and later as Head of the Iranian Central Bank. Having achieved a Doctorate d'Etat from France, Dr. Molavi enjoyed an enviable reputation and maintained an interest in world affairs until his recent death in England, where he had lived for a number of years. I was honored to have been a guest in his home in England for lunch some three years before his death. Like his father, Dr. Molavi was always open to frank discussions and quite ready to listen and consider others' ideas.

I didn't have the pleasure of becoming acquainted with Mahin's father. He passed away shortly after Mahin returned from Iran to the U.S. in 1960. I do know he received his undergraduate degree from the University of Heidelberg in Germany after traveling by boat down the Volga River to reach his desired destination. Upon his return to Iran from Germany, he supposedly became an employee of the Ministry of Foreign Affairs, but apparently like his son Nemat, he never really became active in the ministry.

The members of the Molavi family readily accepted me as one of their own and continue to keep in touch either by telephone or e-mail. I have, however, lost touch with many members of the younger generation because of the diaspora that followed the Islamic Revolution. I hope the members of the new generation continue many of the family traditions of scholarship, adaptability and integrity that I admired in their forefathers.

Like many Persian families, my adopted family learned to live with uncertainty and a lack of trust in their own and foreign governments. They trust primarily those individuals they get to know well and are accepted into their family.

The family is extremely important in Persian culture and I was very fortunate to have the opportunity to be accepted as a member of a wonderful family far different from my own.

Chapter 15

>>>))){{{<<<

Fathering Two Daughters

Mahin and I waited for nine years after our marriage to think about having children, but finally we yielded to the desire to build a legacy for ourselves and enrich our lives through the dreams and hopes of children. The result was the birth of two beautiful daughters: Ladan and Rana.

The births of our two daughters in 1968 and 1973, however, made me realize I hadn't just dipped my toe into a complicated reality but had dived into totally uncharted, unexplored waters. I had never been around children prior to parenting Ladan and Rana, having been raised as an only child. I knew almost nothing about a father's role in relation to a daughter. I wasn't sure how to go about interacting successfully with my daughters even when they were infants. They represented gifts that challenged me and my limited ability to love and be loved.

Looking back now, I can see I could have been caricatured as the clueless father, not knowing what to do with my daughters as they rushed past me on their ways to adventures I didn't and perhaps never understood. When they rolled their eyes at my naiveté, I most often didn't catch on. If they wanted alone time with me, I often didn't know what to do or how to respond.

In retrospect, I realize I wasn't the kind of father to sit with my daughters and play games or cut out pictures from popular magazines. Admittedly, I failed to spend a lot of concentrated, quality time with them while they were growing up. When they were very young, I struggled to see the world through their eyes. I loved them and my feelings toward them were often very complex even to me. I longed to ensure they had roots and desired to give them wings at the appropriate time but didn't always know how to do either. It was my ultimate desire to do no damage to their psyches.

Mahin, I am certain, realized my inability to interact readily with Ladan and Rana, but she never criticized me for my shortcomings. She always reasoned with me concerning the difficulties I experienced in my father-daughter relations and attempted to explain how I might improve the relationships in a very upbeat and non-threatening manner.

Both Ladan and Rana were born in Tehran and held dual citizenships. Their heritage was multicultural: Azarbaijani, Iranian, Arkansan and Californian with some British heritage from my side. They heard at least three languages spoken regularly from birth: Persian, Turkish and English. The environment into which they were born was a complicated mixture of the various cultures.

Usually, a daughter's first love is her father and the relationship a daughter has with her father greatly affects her later life. As I consider the role I played during Ladan's and Rana's maturation process, I have to admit that I probably didn't interact with either daughter enough to be considered their "first love." At the time Mahin and I were raising our daughters, many Iranian fathers seemed to take a more-or-less hands-off approach to the child-raising duties, particularly with girls, and left the nurturing to others. Since I had never been around children and had spent much of my childhood with older people, I comfortably adopted the Iranian approach to child rearing.

I myself had not experienced a close father-son or mother-son relationship. Dad had been emotionally unavailable to me and Mother pretty much kept her feelings and emotions to herself. As a result of my childhood experiences, I shied away from close inter-action with either Ladan or Rana, not knowing what to do and not wanting to hurt them the way I had been psychologically disturbed in childhood. I loved both of them very much and didn't wish to hurt them in any way. I did not want to intervene in situations in which I had little or no experience.

The Islamic Revolution in Iran resulted in a sit-uation that strained whatever relations I had developed with both Ladan and Rana. I had to hide out in Iran to keep from becoming one of the U.S. Embassy hostages and really could not interact with them while in hiding.

From my shelter in Iran, I was forced to leave for the United States without Mahin or the girls. Their dual citizenships permitted them some latitude with the Government of Iran, but my U.S. citizenship placed me in considerable jeopardy. The pain of leaving them haunted me tremendously. I feared for their safety and longed for the day we would reunite.

Our return to the United States from Iran following the revolution made our family, for all practical purposes, a stateless group. We wished for and sought help from the U.S. Government and the International Court in The Hague, but help was never forthcoming. We lost more than a million dollars because of the revolution and felt the U.S. Government was at least partially responsible for our loss. The lawsuit we filed yielded only some $50,000.

Ladan and Rana were eleven and six, respectively, when our family retreated to the United States. Since neither Mahin nor I could find a job, we became depressed and fearful; communication with our daughters was minimal. Our primary family objective was survival. I had little concern about or patience for communication. Both Mahin and I attempted to hide our fear of the future from our girls, but I am certain that our concern was evident to both of them.

We immediately enrolled both girls in public schools in Santa Rosa, California upon our arrival in the United States, and for the first two or three months after their enrollment I had few worries about them. When Ladan entered the seventh grade, however, I sensed a troubling change in her personality and interaction with the family, particularly with me. She developed an attitude of rebellion and seemed to avoid me as much as possible. She wouldn't talk with me unless she had to and preferred to be with her friends or alone. Perhaps this behavior was normal for a teenager, but I feared she was becoming involved with drugs and individuals who would influence her negatively. This fear greatly added to my insecurity and depression and tended to prevent me from communicating in any way with her.

"Do you sense a change in Ladan?" I asked Mahin one morning. "She won't really talk with me or interact with me in any way."

"I have noticed a change," Mahin replied. "But I figure that is just part of being a teenager and one stage of growing up."

"I hope you're right, but I'm afraid she's into something she doesn't want us to know about. I have to see what I can find out."

Each morning Ladan would leave for school, which was perhaps a mile from the small condominium we had purchased, and before she could get two blocks from the condo, I would be in the car following her. She would attempt to ditch me, and I am certain that at times she was successful in doing so. I would intensify my efforts to make sure that she went directly to the school.

After school, the routine would be very much the same. She wouldn't want me to pick her up from school, but I would do my best to follow her from the school to the condo.

After one or two weeks of my sleuthing, Ladan discovered what I was doing and made every effort to find ways of going to and from school that prevented me from easily following her. I remember one day that she ducked into the entrance of a series of apartments and hid somewhere among the plants until I gave up and drove home. To say the least, she didn't like being followed.

This investigative-style routine occupied most of my time for one academic year. Then Mahin and I decided to enroll her in a private school and we both came to feel that was one of the best decisions we made in relation to her education and personality development. She seemed to settle into a different school environment with ease and her behavior became more predictable. She graduated from the prestigious San Domenico High School in Marin County. Throughout her school career she never took her studies very seriously, but in the private schools she did study enough to get decent grades.

Before enrolling Ladan in San Domenico, Mahin attempted to talk with her about attending college after her high school graduation. The conversation went something like this:

"Won't you even think of enrolling in college?" Mahin asked. "After all, a college education is important to your dad and me."

"No," Ladan replied. "I am not interested in going to college. Just because you and Dad got your degrees doesn't mean that I need to."

"Okay," her mom said. "Please do finish San Domenico, and I won't insist that you go to college since you're dead set against it."

To my knowledge, Mahin never mentioned college to Ladan again.

Prior to her graduation from San Domenico, Ladan met a tall, handsome athlete and became infatuated with him. I didn't get to know the young man well but realized early on that we had lost our daughter to him. He had no interest in communicating with Mahin and me and seemed to pull Ladan away from us. Her behavior toward Mahin and me reminded us of the days we endured soon after our return to the U.S. when she would not interact with us.

Soon after her graduation from high school, Ladan broke our hearts by moving in with the young man. Neither Mahin nor I could reconcile ourselves to the lifestyle we assumed she and her partner were living; communication with her became almost impossible. In fact, I almost gave up on reestablishing any type of communication or relationship with her. I feared our older daughter had left us forever.

After several months of sharing an apartment, Ladan and the young man decided to get married. But interaction with her or the new husband remained extremely difficult. His ideas and opinions always took precedence over anything Mahin or I might say about even the least significant topic. We were more or less told to keep our ideas to ourselves. Visits with them were strained.

About two years after announcing her marriage to the young man, Ladan disclosed that the couple had decided to divorce. Following the divorce, I made every effort to entice Ladan to work toward a bachelor's degree. I thought the failed marriage might awaken her to the importance of a college education. But to no avail. She had no interest in attending college. She never said "no" directly to my entreaties, but neither did she say "yes." She more or less ignored me, thereby confirming what she had told her mother several years earlier.

During my campaign to entice her to enroll in a college-degree program, Ladan announced that she had met another young man whom she wanted to marry. What a surprise! Both Mahin and I assumed that she had suffered enough under the first marriage that she would give herself some time before embarking on another marital adventure, but we were wrong.

She was determined to marry Sam Brabo, a college graduate and long-time resident of Marin County.

After several months of courtship, they married. I participated in the wedding ceremony, which occurred in Marin County, but I was not welcomed as a member of the inner circle during the celebration that followed the ceremony. I felt completely ignored and unwanted. My existence seemed more an embarrassment than a blessing. I was certain that neither the son-in-law nor his parents liked me or wanted to have anything to do with me.

Years of poor communication and uncertain relationships followed. Several children were born; I never felt I was a part of their lives. I remained a stranger, a detached family member, trying to look in from the outside. In my opinion, I was "Papa Frank" in name only.

Both Ladan and Sam, however, became increasingly engaged in church and spiritual matters. As their spiritual lives took shape, communication with both of them became easier. Eventually, we came to have much in common: spiritual topics and ideas that we could readily discuss and share. Gradually, our daughter returned to us with a husband with whom we could interact and feel comfortable. Ladan and Sam as well as the five children continue to be blessings to me. I cherish our time together and enjoy observing them interacting as a family I'm so grateful to have to this day.

Unlike Ladan, Rana had a difficult time adjusting to private schools. She attended public schools through the early elementary grades, but when we moved from Santa Rosa to San Rafael, Mahin and I enrolled her in the San Rafael Mission School. She expressed dislike for the school within a few weeks and we kept her there for only one academic year. When we temporarily moved from San Rafael to Tiburon, we enrolled her in a public middle school and she expressed extreme satisfaction with the school. In Walnut Creek, she attended a public middle school and graduated from Northgate High School.

Having obtained her high school diploma, Rana decided to attend Diablo Valley College (DVC), the local community college in Pleasant Hill. She took a break from her studies to spend a year in Paris, where she studied French and broadened her multicultural experience. I accompanied her and helped her settle in before returning to the U.S. and had the pleasure of visiting with her during the Christmas holidays while she was there. Mahin also visited her; together they travelled to the south of France where we had in earlier years spent several summers. She lived at home during her time at the college, and Mahin and I greatly enjoyed our interaction with her.

From DVC she transferred to San Francisco State University (SFSU) to work toward a Bachelor of Arts degree in International Relations. For the first twelve to eighteen months at SFSU, she seemed content to live at home, but later she expressed a strong desire to move to San Francisco and openly declared that Mahin and I should rent her an apartment in the city. The monthly rent would have approached $2,000, and we felt that such a sum was a bit much for us. Also, she was attending classes only three days per week. Why couldn't she continue to live at home until after graduation?

I left the negotiations with Rana regarding the apartment to Mahin, and the exchange of words became rather strong and sometimes bitter.

"Why don't you want to rent an apartment for me in the city?" Rana asked.

"Because we don't have the wherewithal to pay some $2,000 each month, particularly when you are attending classes only three days each week," Mahin would answer.

"You just don't want me to live independently. I want to be on my own," Rana would retort.

And the argument would go on and on.

Shortly after her graduation from SFSU, Rana asked her brother-in-law, Sam and me to move her to San Mateo. She left our home with a great deal of bitterness and an apparent determination to prevent us from interacting with her. She seemed to feel we had not been fair to her and had denied her the right to an apartment during her time at SFSU. She had no contact with us for almost nine years, a period of time that

149

was extremely difficult for both Mahin and me but especially for Mahin. It was nine years of sheer limbo.

During the years of estrangement, Mahin and I lived about eighteen months in San Mateo close to where I was serving at Notre Dame de Namur University. I can recall two heartbreaking incidents in which I saw Rana but didn't dare attempt to communicate with her. Once I was taking a walk in the evening and spied her in a local deli. I could hardly contain myself but didn't dare approach her alone. I couldn't bear being ignored. I ran home to inform Mahin that I had seen Rana from a distance and that she seemed to be quite healthy. Both Mahin and I rushed back to the deli to catch a glimpse of our estranged daughter, but by the time we reached the shopping center, which was right next to our condominium, Rana had disappeared.

Mahin and I were very depressed for the next two days. We could hardly sleep at night, and the walks we took almost every day were plagued by silence. Neither one of us would talk other than bemoaning the fact that I had seen Rana but didn't have the courage to speak to her.

The night after spying Rana at the deli, Mahin asked me, "What do you think we can do to reconnect with Rana?"

"I have no idea," I answered. "I am afraid to make the first move. I fear further rejection."

"We need to think of something," Mahin said. "This long separation is really weighing on my nerves and health."

I had no answer. I could only pray.

The second incident occurred at Barnes and Noble Book Store in San Mateo. I was researching a particular subject one evening and was just leaving the facility when I looked out of my car window and saw Rana entering the bookstore. I didn't attempt to approach her but merely sat deflated and wondered what we had done so wrong to lose a daughter with apparently no opportunity of reigniting any type of love or affection. Again, I feared rejection.

Following my departure from the University and our period of residency in San Mateo, we returned to Walnut Creek, but once every two or three weeks Mahin and I would get in the car, drive to San Mateo and pass the home where we knew she was living. We had engaged the services of an investigator to find the correct address. We eventually spied her through the front window of the home late one night. How thrilled we were!

Rana moved from the house with which we had become familiar, and we could not discover her new address for a while. Finally, we engaged a private detective who discovered the new address and began to follow her and record her goings and comings, particularly to and from her place of work. We were concerned that she might not be working and did not want her to be without some type of income.

Our concern about Rana's well being was a totally separate consideration from our estranged relationship. She was still our daughter, and we did not want her to be without the necessities of life. We still loved her very much and wanted to help in whatever way we could.

The detective did his work for some time and finally during a Christmas holiday he attempted to deliver a Christmas gift from us to her in the form of a check. She didn't respond well to our gesture and let us know in no uncertain terms through the detective that she wasn't interested in interacting with us in any way.

This virtual standoff continued for an extended period of time; finally Mahin took the initiative and telephoned Rana.

"What might help in healing wounds and begin the rebuilding of a relationship?" Mahin asked.

"A start would be the purchase of a Louis Vuitton laptop carrying case," Rana answered.

"All right," her mom responded. "Where can I find one?"

Rana gave the name of a store in San Francisco that had the kind of case she wanted. The next day Mahin and I took BART to San Francisco and purchased the case, which was sent by mail to Rana's address.

Once again Mahin and Rana talked by telephone. I listened carefully to the one side of the conversation I could hear and was pleased. It seemed the two had been able to make some progress in establishing a new line of communication. The actual standoff between Rana and us, however, continued until the day before Mahin's death.

Rana appeared at John Muir Hospital the day before the doctors disconnected Mahin from the life-sustaining equipment and spent the night beside her mom. I discovered her presence at the hospital the next morning when I attempted to enter the room where Mahin was lying and was denied entrance. When I inquired as to the reason for the denial, I was told my daughter was with her mother and preferred not to see me. To say the least, I was devastated. I was losing my wife but could not enter the room to visit with her prior to her imminent death because my estranged daughter did not want to see me. I wanted nothing more than to be at my dearly beloved wife's side but respected Rana's wishes.

I proceeded to the waiting room where I sat for a while and then decided to go home and return after an hour or so. As I was leaving the hospital, I suddenly came face-to-face with Rana. Initially, she didn't seem interested in even saying 'hello' to me, but after some uncertain moments, she agreed to sit down and talk. That conversation was, at first, awkward, but groundbreaking nevertheless.

"How have you been?" I asked.

"I am doing all right," Rana answered.

"How did you find out about your mom's condition?" I inquired.

"Ladan telephoned me," she responded.

"I'm sorry you had to visit your mom under these circumstances but I do appreciate you coming," I offered. "I hope we can get together soon."

From that time until now, she and I have gradually developed a relationship that allows us to interact while making certain that we do not intrude on each other's territory. I am very thankful for Rana's willingness to make an effort to communicate with me. She has become very dear to me.

I often marvel at her intelligence and thoroughly enjoy just being with her. Her suggestions regarding many things in life are well thought out and very practical. She often acts as a counselor when I have no one else in whom I can confide.

Life involves beginnings and endings. The beginning stage with my two daughters occurred in an Iranian-influenced setting that may have limited my understanding of them and my ability to imbue them with confidence and assertive energy. Perhaps I failed to encourage them to develop a commitment toward me or stay connected. I feel certain the role I played in their lives when they were children and young adults didn't encourage them to look on me as the first love in their lives. Perhaps I didn't listen enough, value their opinions sufficiently or ask for their input regarding family issues as frequently as I should have.

It is my hope, however, that my passivity didn't cause any psychological damage to my daughters. I certainly didn't perpetrate any physical abuse. I hope that I didn't diminish their self-worth. If I unknowingly caused any harm to them, I apologize and ask for forgiveness.

I often wish I had spent more time with each of them, listening to their thoughts, teaching them new things, having fun, telling them how beautiful they were and writing personal notes. I could have set a better example of manhood for them and perhaps could have given them more confidence.

I would love to view myself through their eyes and know that I am worthy of their love. I want to protect them even more than I did when they were youngsters. In short, I would now like to be their hero.

But I can't wallow in regret. I have a vision for the future and an understanding of where I am today. Ladan and Rana as well as Ladan's husband and children are all included in that vision and understanding. I have traversed the valley of experience in search of a 'self' and a spiritual reality. I am climbing the mountain of hope but have not yet reached the summit where I can gaze on the past, present and future in an instant and thank God for the journey to complete emancipation and perfect wisdom. When I reach the summit of life, my arms will extend upward in praise and will serve as the wings of an eagle, enabling me to fly with the assurance that I am loved and can love in return.

Chapter 16

>>>>))(((<<

Persian Caviar and Russian Vodka:
A Duet to Remember

Like the wetlands of Louisiana, the marsh that
bordered our two-bedroom cottage near the Caspian
Sea was water-saturated and swampy. It glorified itself
with bushes, rushes, cattails and reeds and housed in-
vertebrates, fish and huge frogs but, to my knowledge,
no alligators. Graceful waterfowl soared above the
herbaceous plants, lending a surreal dimension to the
peaceful scene.

The nearby sluggish bayou permitted small
rowboats to navigate the vegetation and fishermen to
farm the fish, bullfrogs and crayfish. This minor braid
of the Volga River channel with its slow-moving
stream and brackish water reminded the onlooker of
an element of southern Cajun culture inadvertently
dropped into the Middle East.

Each time I dreamed about the Volga, often referred to as "Russia's Main Street," I would recall the
story about my father-in-law travelling up the river
from Azarbaijan to Russia and then by land to Germany early in the twentieth century to pursue his degree
in diplomacy at the University of Heidelberg.

Across the narrow highway lay the largest enclosed inland body of water on earth: the Caspian Sea.

The ancient inhabitants of the Caspian area classified the body of water as an ocean; today, oceanographers refer to the Caspian as the world's largest lake or a full-fledged sea. Fishing for sturgeon and the transformation of the salt-cured sturgeon roe into the delicious delicacy referred to as caviar represented major occupations along the Caspian shores.

Several miles up the highway, a traveler would encounter the Soviet border, and reportedly along the highway leading to the border well-concealed listening stations placed in Iran by the Central Intelligence Agency with the permission and support of the Government of Iran would monitor at least some of the goings on within the Soviet Union. A large Iranian construction firm contracted with the CIA for the development of those stations, which might have provided politically-oriented information but could not readily report on the illegal importation of Russian vodka and its sales along the border.

I thoroughly enjoyed relaxing at the Caspian cottage. During the spring and summer, I could lounge on the front porch, view the beautiful marshes and bayous; during the autumn and winter, I would stare into the glowing fireplace and dream. I could also stretch out on the sand or enjoy a mid-day drink at the luxury hotel a few blocks from the cabin. Most often, I would go to the Caspian alone because Mahin preferred to visit Europe or remain in Tehran. Only the driver employed by the U.S. Chamber of Commerce in Tehran accompanied me.

If only I could paint a portrait to depict what I saw. I believe a photograph wouldn't do justice to the breathtaking scene. The expansive clear sky would often permit an unobstructed view of the marsh, the bayou and the Caspian Sea; even when the weather was not clear, the surroundings possessed a mystical and somewhat spiritual quality. With no outlet, the sea loses water only through the process of evaporation; the resulting saltiness and the humidity often reminded me of the Biblical reference to us humans as the salt of the earth, a significant part of God's creation. I was often reminded that like the sea I could receive and retain my blessings. Even though my saltiness might be minimal compared to others, I didn't want to lose it and be forgotten, "thrown out and trampled by men."

The Volga River, until the seventeenth century thought to be an underground spring but now acknowledged as the longest river in Europe, would regularly test my mental agility. I imagined its flow from northwest of Moscow to the Caspian and mentally travelled with the flow, cherishing the ancient sites and natural beauty along the way. It would strike me as an almost mythical stream, touching peoples of diverse cultures and languages. I would attempt to grasp its eighty percent contribution to the Caspian's freshwater inflow. Frequently, I would imaginatively attempt to explore the many tributaries that form its river system.

At times, I would focus on the Caspian, which has no outflows. I would offer thanks that I had mental and social outflows to members of the family and friends who I knew truly cared for me and reciprocated with ease and clarity. I could picture the Romans at the Caspian declaring it a sea because of its saltiness. Had I not known its true oceanographic classification, what seemed to be a far horizon could have encouraged me to compare it to the Atlantic or the Pacific Ocean. No oil or gas production platforms blocked my perspective.

The history ensconced along the shores of the Caspian could prove almost mind-boggling. Stone-age tools have been found along the shores. Both the Russian and Persian cultures date back millennia. Horses may have first been domesticated in steppes along the Caspian, Black and Azov Seas.

Whenever I morphed into a particularly contemplative mood, I would focus on the apparition known as the "Caspian Sea Monster." No, this monster was not of the same genre as the Loch Ness Monster. It was a ground-effect vehicle characterized as a transition between a hovercraft and an aircraft that achieved level flight near the earth's surface.

U.S. spy satellites had photographed the strange aircraft-type creature in the 1960s in Soviet territory and had become extremely intrigued by the aircraft's ability to fly low and lift heavy loads with minimal effort. I tried to imagine what I would do if I saw an object 310 feet long and weighing some 540 tons flying toward me low on the Caspian.

The Soviets continued to experiment with the monster for use as a very high-speed military transport and based it along the shores of the Caspian. I would shudder to think America's nemesis in the Cold War could render my beloved Caspian Sea and me for that matter, helpless and subject to the much-detested Communist way of life. After the collapse of the Soviet Union, Russia began to concentrate on smaller planes of the same type for non-military purposes.

While visiting the Caspian, usually on the weekends, my consumption of frog legs was minimal. I had had an aversion to that delicacy even as a child in the Southern United States. I could just never get the picture of the frog and the sound of the croaking off my mind while trying to down the parts of the body that enable the animal to jump.

But it didn't take me long after arriving in Iran to develop a taste for sturgeon and its salt-cured eggs, particularly the roe from the beluga sturgeon, now about $7000 to $10,000 per two pounds. Pair the eggs with some lemon juice, diced onions and a few crispy crackers, and you're in heaven.

About noon each weekend day I would go out with the driver, cross the highway to the seashore, discover a vendor cooking the sturgeon and purchase enough for our dinners. A little way down the shore, I would spy another vendor selling the caviar and purchase enough of the roe for hors d'oeuvres. We usually brought the crackers with us from Tehran.

From the seashore, the driver would escort me toward the Soviet border where I knew I would find a bottle of vodka that would taste as smooth as velvet and go down my throat like water. Sometimes I couldn't wait until we returned to the cabin to have a snort of the demon juice.

After purchasing the ingredients, the driver and I would return to the cabin and begin an afternoon of leisure. By early evening, both of us were relaxed and ready to sing or just sleep. I easily forgot about the Caspian Sea Monster and the Cold War. We had the duet to remember: Persian caviar and Russian vodka. We were lacking nothing. We were in Caspian heaven.

Chapter 17

>>>>>>))《《《《《

The Powerful vs. the Weak:
A Case of Institutional Discrimination

I heard the news while standing in the reception area of Armstrong University in downtown Berkeley. The Western Association of Schools and Colleges (WASC) had just informed the Board of Directors that the university's accreditation would be revoked unless the Association could be convinced that the university could and would comply with the Association's regulations and standards.

The institution was abuzz with gossip about the news. One very prominent rumor focused on the recently retired owner/president, who had objected openly and formally to the formation of the accrediting agencies in the 1960s. People in the know shared the view that WASC planned to close the institution in retaliation for the owner's opposition to its formation.

Both instructors and support staff feared the loss of their jobs, and so did I. My tenure at the university had been relatively short. I had been serving as an English-as-a-Second Language instructor barely a year and during that year had observed numerous changes that, in my opinion, didn't bode well for the institution. The owner/president suddenly left the post, and in his place the Board of Trustees appointed an attorney to serve as CEO. The attorney's tenure proved ineffective. He couldn't effect reforms or make even small decisions. The Board granted him full authority, but he performed like a political figurehead who holds a prestigious title but has little power.

WASC's announcement concerning the accreditation prompted the Board to dismiss the attorney without identifying a possible replacement. The university had no professional leadership to guide the Board and staff in addressing WASC's concerns.

In an attempt to minimize the fear among the members of the staff, the Board of Directors called a meeting with only non-family board members present. I was eager to learn exactly what was transpiring and so decided to slip into the meeting room, thinking I would not be noticed. Looking around the room, I wondered what the faculty and office staff would do if the institution lost its regional accreditation. I gave thought to what I might personally do.

I pondered the alternatives available to the Board of Directors and the family. They could close the school within a year, fight WASC, apply for national, professional accreditation or undertake a combination of those alternatives.

Halfway through the meeting, the Chair of the Board, who was conducting the meeting turned to me and asked, "Frank, would you consider assuming the presidency? I have consulted with members of the Armstrong family who have worked with you during the past year, and they have been impressed with your ability and willingness to work as a member of a team. I have also talked with several members of the staff who have expressed similar opinions. We need a team builder right now."

I was surprised with the endorsement but pleased. I had never served as the CEO or president of an educational institution. Serving in that position during such uncertain times would be a challenge, but I thought I was ready for a summons to a contest.

I considered the request for several minutes and finally responded, "I am willing to serve as president at least until the institution's future is somewhat clearer. A long-term commitment is less certain."

This response launched me on a rocky, two-year journey that greatly enhanced my professional experience but also labeled me as an "academic loser." In 2001, the website known as DegreeInfo (www.DegreeInfo.com) commented online that I "presided over Armstrong University when it lost accreditation." The operators of the website did not take the time to discover my effort at saving the small institution from the attack of the giant known as WASC by obtaining national accreditation. The website preferred to emphasize the negative over whatever positive accomplishments I made during my presidency.

To provide some historical perspective, I joined Armstrong as an instructor in the late-1980s, about seventy years after its establishment. J. Evan Armstrong founded the institution in 1918 under the name California School for Private Secretaries. The classes met in the old First National Bank Building in Berkeley, California. Its popularity resulted in a move from its original headquarters. The school grew rapidly, and it eventually moved from its original building to the UC Theater Building on University Avenue.

Ultimately, the school became known as the Armstrong School of Business or Armstrong College and moved to a Spanish Colonial style building on Harold Way. Armstrong College became Armstrong University in the late-1980s and maintained that designation until its demise in the mid-1990s. I assumed the presidency of the school in 1988, shortly after the designation change.

The City of Berkeley declared the building on Harold Way a landmark in 1994, and Armstrong University continued to operate out of that building until 1996. In that year the university apparently sold the right to operate to another group, vacated the building and rented it to the University of California for use as a training center. A website which focuses on historical sites states that Tibetan Nyingma Mediation Center bought the building in 2009 and renamed it the Dharma College.

Accreditation of institutions of higher learning in the United States began as early as the 1960s as a movement to ensure the quality of programs of study and appease the federal government. The United

States Department of Education recognizes only agencies dealing with institutions of higher education. The quality of elementary and secondary education is determined or monitored by the various states.

The elevation of private associations and commissions to the level of institutional judges seemed to disturb the founder of Armstrong College. He foresaw the possibility of prejudice and institutional discrimination in the operation of such organizations. Through his testimony, he demonstrated a willingness to expose himself and his school to retribution in an effort to avoid such a possibility.

My experience with WASC while serving as President of Armstrong confirmed the possibility of institutional discrimination. I found that the Association was far stricter with the small, less prestigious institutions than with the well-known colleges and universities. I came to attribute that strictness to the smaller institutions' lack of influence and prestige.

According to published materials, the accrediting process is strictly voluntary. By accepting accreditation an institution of higher education "agrees to uphold the quality standards set" by the accrediting body. Periodically, an accredited institution must submit to a renewal review by unbiased groups and/or individuals recognized by the accrediting agency.

The accreditation process is, at least as it applied to Armstrong, comprised of essentially five steps: preparation and self-examination; peer review; visit and examination by peers from other institutions; judgment action made by the accrediting organization; and, continuous review. The first step requires the college or university to prepare materials that show the institution's accomplishments and compose a written report of those accomplishments within the accrediting agency's framework.

The second step involves an intensive review of the institution's report by outside administrators and faculty peers and a campus visit by the peer group; it is at this juncture in the process that troubles can begin. Often peers from major colleges and universities measure small institutions against the larger institutions or the institutions from which they come. If the smaller, less prestigious institutions fail to meet or vary from the peer standards, those institutions probably will not be evaluated positively and may be asked to establish policies, procedures and/or structures really not appropriate to them. In the case of Armstrong's evaluation, I did not feel the review contained any objectivity, nor were the suggested "upgrades" necessarily appropriate for the university. Herein lies a major quandary. To what extent should a smaller institution forego its uniqueness to comply with demands from an outside peer group or organization quite unfamiliar with the campus milieu and population? To what extent do the outsiders' demands focus on standards rather than personal or organizational preferences?

Following the peer review and visit, an additional team of peers may be formed and asked to gather information and further evaluate the institution. I don't recall this particular step having been taken in the case of Armstrong during my presidency.

Once the foregoing steps have been accomplished, the accrediting organization, in this case WASC, asks its commission to review the information and affirm or deny accreditation to the institution or put the institution on probation. The WASC commission found Armstrong wanting and placed it on probation. A certain amount of time was granted to make the suggested corrections, but even when the commission announced the probationary period for the necessary institutional corrections, it was quite evident that accreditation would ultimately be denied, no matter what the university attempted to correct and improve within the framework of WASC's demands.

After being placed on probation, Armstrong made every effort to comply with WASC's suggestions and requests. I worked closely with faculty committees and other administrators in an effort to correct the perceived inadequacies. The committees and I met frequently with WASC officers, hosted a number of formal lunches to discuss the requested changes and made a monumental effort to comply with what I came to refer to as the list of WASC complaints.

Our efforts, however, proved to be of no avail. Each time we approached the agency, the school was castigated, and we were told that we had not met even the basic requirements for accreditation. I gradually realized that no matter what we did, Armstrong would not be granted a continuation of its regional accreditation. I, therefore, began to investigate the possibility of obtaining national, professional accreditation. Such accreditation would not be as prestigious as that provided by WASC but would enable the school to function, albeit in a more limited way.

During the time Armstrong was attempting to renew its accreditation, I had the opportunity to observe a WASC employee interact with a University of California, Berkeley administrator and discover the approach the Association took with that prestigious university. One day I was having lunch with the vice-president of the university and discussing certain matters of interest to Armstrong in its relationship to the university. During that lunch, one of the WASC officers approached the vice president concerning the university's accreditation. Rather than approaching the vice-president in the demanding manner he usually approached me, he was almost apologetic that he had to disturb the vice-president. The officer asked several questions, and the vice-president responded in no uncertain terms as to what the university would and would not do.

The WASC officer did not respond to the vice-president and seemed to accept what he had been told. No demands. No arguments. No strong statements to the effect that the university had to do certain things to comply with WASC standards. The university, it seemed, was able to dictate to WASC what it would and would not do.

After listening to the brief conversation between the university vice-president and the WASC officer, my thought was this: WASC is biased against small, struggling institutions. Large institutions can pretty well dictate what they will do and pay minimal attention to the accrediting agencies, but the smaller, less prestigious institutions must adhere strictly to the agency demands and standards and dare not frustrate the agencies by declaring independence.

Granted, experts in higher-education will declare that the major universities need less supervision and critiquing than do the smaller institutions, but I believe the accrediting agencies sometimes make excessive demands of the smaller colleges and universities and attempt to make them into entities which do not and cannot fulfill the purposes for which they were founded.

While still attempting to fulfill the demands WASC was making on Armstrong, I approached a national accrediting agency regarding accreditation. The agency sent a team of peers who followed essentially the same process that WASC had adhered to. The team gave the university a positive evaluation and within weeks, Armstrong had national, professional accreditation.

A short time after Armstrong achieved its professional accreditation, I left the presidency and was succeeded by the gentleman who had served as vice-president during my tenure. I am unaware how long the latter gentleman remained president.

My presidency of Armstrong proved rocky and uncertain from the outset. Not only did WASC look askance at every move the faculty and I made and severely criticize almost every attempt to comply with their demands, the Armstrong family and board members seemed conflicted. It often seemed the family was ready to close the school and move on. Most board members didn't appear to value accreditation. Perhaps the family and board members were simply tired of battling WASC. WASC also seemed to be determined to strip Armstrong of any academic legitimacy.

In many ways, the accrediting agencies can be viewed as oligarchies. They too often involve small groups of educators who view themselves as academic missionaries sent to convert or destroy small institutions of higher education. In their own opinions they represent the "intellectual and cultural elite." In the opinion of many of them, they enjoy intellectual hegemony.

To me, Armstrong had a potential role in higher education that larger institutions could not assume or fulfill. Students from countries around the world were attracted to Armstrong and benefitted greatly from the personal training and attention they received. They were not just numbers but members of a developing global society. The dissolution of the weak with such potential by associations catering to the more academically elite institutions seemed, and still seems, unfair and worthy of mention in writing.

My experience at Armstrong drove me temporarily into my figurative Pepper Tree Kingdom and raised a number of questions for me. I could not readily identify with the "intellectual elite" who had so easily turned aside the tremendous and, in my opinion, fruitful efforts of the Armstrong administration, faculty and staff. I could not reconcile what appeared to me to be a WASC incongruity of denying Armstrong membership in the regional academic club while not providing an adequate recourse for Armstrong to challenge the denial of membership. WASC's actions and belittling approach smacked of dictatorship and deliberate exclusion, neither of which I viewed as truly American.

The two questions that kept haunting me were these:

1. How could the oligarchy of accrediting agencies be democratized?
2. Why could an inclusive accrediting organization that operated internationally not be established and made operational?

I decided to experiment with a globally-oriented accrediting agency, one that would make every effort to be inclusive while encouraging quality and a minimum level of standardization. An emphasis would be on the accreditation of what might be termed "the global university," an institution that did not have formal classrooms. The experiment seemed exciting and promising. Little did I realize at the time that the formation of the agency would prove to be a major academic stumble.

Chapter 18

>>>))((<<<

Playing the Real Estate Developer Role

Before returning to the U.S. following the Islamic Revolution, I never considered becoming a real estate developer. That profession seemed totally foreign to me and my background. I was, at least I thought, primarily wired for academia.

Imagine my surprise then when a mere acquaintance, Mr. William (Bill) Black approached me to work with him on a multi-million dollar development project involving the construction of a series of condominiums.

It was the early 1980s. Interest rates were skyrocketing, limiting the sale of single-family homes. But the prospects of benefitting from the development and sale of multi-family units appeared promising.

Mahin and I had lost more than one million dollars just prior to our departure from Iran, and any prospects for employment in our own fields seemed negligible. I was cooperating with a group of Iranians in San Francisco who suffered tremendous financial losses because of the Islamic Revolution and could offer only a minimum wage. The family and I needed some cash merely to exist, and Bill's proposal struck me as a Godsend.

Bill had successfully developed several projects and invited me to join with him, partially because of my activities and the contacts I had developed during my first two years in Santa Rosa, California. Soon after settling in Santa Rosa, I began to work closely with the Republican Central Committee for Sonoma County and soon found myself in charge of the County Election Headquarters. Bill had been impressed with my apparent connections and decided to invite me to work with him, thinking the connections could benefit the proposed project.

Bill possessed considerable knowledge in most of the development processes. He had renovated existing buildings, purchased and sold undeveloped land and converted ideas into real property. He had obtained approval and financing for a number of projects. He had worked with architects, city planners, engineers, inspectors, contractors and leasing agents. He had played crucial roles in the formation of a number of physical environments. His weakness, according to his own admission, was interpersonal relations.

In contrast, my strengths lay in the human relations area. I also understood contracts and the concerns related to liability. Together we were certain we could do well. We agreed to form a small firm under the name Woodlake Properties.

In our initial conversation concerning the formation of Woodlake Properties, Bill asked, "Frank, are you interested in joining me in a real estate development project which looms large on the horizon? I can handle the multifaceted technical side, but I often run into difficulties when faced with interpersonal challenges."

"Bill, I have never worked as a developer and have never thought of playing such a role, but if you can handle the development side of the work, I am certainly willing to use my communication skills to our advantage," I said.

"I'm impressed with the way you become acquainted and work with a variety of people. I have watched your skills at work for several weeks now and have read about your political activities in Sonoma County. You haven't been here long, but a lot of people already know and respect you," Bill offered.

"Thank you for the compliment. I hope I can meet your expectations in developing the project. I will certainly do my best," I responded. "Incidentally, what is the project you are proposing?"

"It is a condominium project I hope we can build in Bennett Valley," Bill stated. "The land is available and centrally located. All we need to do is get the financing, and that seems quite possible."

We shook hands and proceeded to form Woodlake Properties.

Mahin had been aware of the possible partnership with Bill from the beginning of our conversation, and she seemed to approve of my potential new role.

"Frank, you will probably get a decent salary for your work during the construction phase of the project and the income likely from the sale of the units should get us out of our financial straits," she pointed out one day. "For the first time since we arrived in Santa Rosa, I feel upbeat."

I was ecstatic that she felt so positive and took her upbeat attitude as a sign of the eventual success of the project.

"I will do my best and will call on you at times. You have a very good sense of business. Together, we can work with Bill and ensure that everyone benefits from our efforts," I offered.

Bill and I hired a well-known, very competent, San Francisco attorney to form the corporation and guide us through the legal jungle associated with any major project. We knew we would need legal advice and assistance until the last condominium was sold, but we had no idea of the amount of advice and guidance we would require before the end of the project.

Shortly after establishing Woodlake and submitting an offer on the plot of land Bill had discovered, we approached two savings and loans (S&Ls), the type of banking institution very popular at the time. We chose Centennial Savings and Loan headquartered in Santa Rosa, a savings and loan that received not only much attention but also much adulation.

Bill and I understood that S&Ls were specialized banks formed to promote affordable home ownership. The majority of homebuyers obtained their mortgages through S&Ls throughout the 1960s and 1970s, but by the 1980s money-market accounts had begun to erode the attractiveness of the S&Ls. This erosion and pressure from the industry prompted the U.S. Congress to relax the restrictions imposed on the institutions until the 1980s.

We were not, however, aware that the relaxation of restrictions allowed the S&Ls to invest in perilous ventures, which, at least partially, led to the S&L crisis. The absolutely positive image Centennial enjoyed in the Santa Rosa area discouraged any thought of risky investments, corruption or overspending by that institution.

We put our team together rather quickly and began the project. We progressed without many interruptions or organizational setbacks, but about halfway through the project, we discovered that the U.S. government was investigating Centennial.

According to Douglas Frantz, the staff writer for the Los Angeles Times, the president of Centennial and a prominent developer in Santa Rosa not only invested in risky ventures but also spent exorbitant amounts of Centennial's money for personal pleasure. They bought useless projects for vast sums of money, took long, expensive trips and paid themselves large salaries and bonuses. They even sold Centennial a poorly kept Santa Rosa landmark known as The Stonehouse. Their spending seemed to have no limits.

We gradually became aware of the antics of Centennial's officers and asked our attorney to help us initiate a lawsuit against Centennial. We had hesitated about filing a suit but gradually decided we had no choice.

Bill and I met at a local restaurant in Santa Rosa one weekday for lunch and began to discuss the situation at Centennial.

"I am worried we may lose our project," Bill pined. "I don't want to file a lawsuit but am beginning to believe we need to do so if we want to get anything for our efforts."

I thought for a few minutes, mulling the amount of work I realized would be involved in a lawsuit. Finally, I agreed.

"I guess you're right, Bill. I dread the work and the confrontation with the Centennial officers, but I don't think we have a choice. Let's instruct the attorney to file the suit."

We followed through, and the outcome looked promising for Woodlake Properties. Centennial officers really couldn't defend their behavior, and the extravagance of their actions was well known by then.

We were making considerable headway in our case against Centennial when the U.S. Government decided it had to take over the institution. The government action preempted the continuation of our legal action; we weren't allowed to sue the U.S. Government.

With the government takeover, Bill asked me if I would become the President of Woodlake Properties and work with our attorney and a second legal hire in an attempt to reach a settlement with the government. I reluctantly accepted the position and the associated tasks.

"Bill, I am not certain I can keep up with the responsibilities inherent in the law suit," I expressed to Bill one day when he was insisting that I become President of the company.

"Frank, you are the only one that will follow through. I will support you in every way possible, but I know myself. I get tired quickly and give up too easily. Remember I'm not in good health. Please do this for me. If you will do it, we can get at least something for our efforts."

"Okay, Bill. I will do it for you even though I don't really want the headache," I said.

For months, I worked almost night and day. I acquainted myself with legal terminology and processes in which I had no knowledge or even interest. Finally, we reached a settlement, which provided some profit but not the windfall we had hoped for.

Once we had reached a settlement, I decided, with Bill's consent, to dissolve Woodlake Properties. The dissolution occurred on October 31, 1983. We celebrated Halloween as former owners of a development firm. Our 'Nightmare on Elm Street' was finally over.

The role as an entrepreneur was for me an eye opener. I learned a lot and took some hard knocks. The experience, however, held me in good stead when one of my MBA students at Notre Dame de Namur University from the Philippines asked me if I could and would work with him in hotel development in an effort to secure his U.S. permanent visa.

I put forth considerable effort on behalf of the student, whom the United States welcomed as an investor with his $500,000 plus. Together we formed a team, bought and sold the historical hotel in Paso Robles, California and eventually purchased the historical hotel in Monterey, California. I sold my share of the Monterey hotel in the late 1990s.

The United States represented the student's first choice for investment. He and his family were ready to chance a dream. I was privileged to play a role in helping them realize that dream. I felt proud that I helped at least one family of international entrepreneurs reach their goal in their adopted homeland.

Chapter 19

>>>))(((<<

An Attempted Educational Outreach: Teaming up With an Atlantis Researcher

In the early 1990s, a representative of the California Department of Education introduced me to a Dr. Green. The representative knew of my unrewarding experience with the education establishment in relation to Armstrong University and my naive interest in experimenting with a substitute accrediting and higher-education structure; the representative presented Dr. Green as a strong, intelligent potential partner in such an endeavor. According to the representative, Dr. Green was an ardent researcher regarding the lost continent Atlantis.

I knew almost nothing about lost continents, but their possible existence had long intrigued me. I had only heard the name "Mu" as well as the name "Atlantis." "Mu" had supposedly existed in one of the Earth's oceans prior to the beginning of human history. "Atlantis" had received much attention but to me remained merely a figment of the imagination.

A preliminary search of Dr. Green's background revealed an extremely intelligent and innovative individual. Public records showed that she had convinced my alma mater, Pepperdine University, to sponsor an expedition to search for "Atlantis." She conducted the expedition and declared it a success. She and members of her expedition claimed to have discovered and photographed artifacts of the continent. Media coverage of the expedition included articles in major journals. Dr. Green herself had written or co-written two or more books about the lost continent.

Dr. Green boasted a strong academic background. She had earned three degrees from well-known U.S. institutions and a second doctorate from a European university, but very impressive to me was her distrust of the educational establishment. I shared her apparent dislike of accrediting agencies because of the way the Western Association of Schools and Colleges had dealt with Armstrong University and the agency's apparent complete servitude to major universities like the University of California, Berkeley.

During a brief telephone call, we discussed our adventures in several countries and agreed that interacting with a variety of cultures made life very interesting. A short in-person visit convinced me Dr. Green represented the intellectual community well.

"I like to experiment with ideas," Dr. Green declared. "I would rather try something and find it doesn't work than sit idly by. For that reason, I would like to establish a distance-learning institution accessible to interested individuals around the world. And I don't necessarily want the traditional accrediting agencies involved."

"I feel the same way," I responded. "And I am convinced that accrediting agencies do not want experimentation. They only want conformity. Why not establish an international body?"

I felt I had found a professional soul mate in this sixty-five plus academician. Like me, Dr. Green had seen the world. She showed ambition and determination. Her fibromyalgia didn't seem to slow her down. Her mind dictated to her body rather than the reverse. After a few weeks, we joined forces by setting up an accrediting organization primarily for institutions outside the United States. We also did the groundwork for an online degree-granting institution.

The first few months went quite well. We arranged a conference in New York and invited several speakers from the U.S. Government to participate. Educators from various countries also attended. Membership in the recently established accrediting agency began to grow.

Through some fluke, a Saudi Arabia prince approached Dr. Green concerning the possibility of earning a degree for himself and offered to pay our ways first-class to Jeddah for consultation and getting-acquainted sessions. The trip was planned for the first part of December with a three-or-four day pause in Paris, France. My younger daughter was living in Paris at the time, and I was delighted to be able to spend some time with her.

Our arrival at the Jeddah airport proved auspicious. As soon as the plane had parked and the passengers had begun to disembark, an airport official appeared in the cabin and called our names. Before we could actually identify ourselves, the official ushered us out of the airplane into a waiting limousine, which rushed us to a private terminal. There our papers were quickly processed, and we were on our way to the hotel.

Each of our suites at the hotel was as large as an apartment, with every amenity imaginable. For the several nights we were in Jeddah, I would wander from room to room in my suite prior to going to bed and think about the cost of such a facility. For some time, I had travelled first class by air and had enjoyed the luxury of staying in major hotels, but I had never been exposed to facilities as elaborate and elegant as those in which I found myself during that particular trip.

The prince and his private assistant became very friendly with me, and for several years we kept in close touch. I arranged for the prince's son to attend the then-College of Notre Dame in Belmont, California, and the prince co-authored with me a volume of essays entitled *The World of Learning*. He even visited with me in San Francisco at one point. For several years now, however, I have not been able to reconnect with him or his assistant and have no idea what happened to them. The relationship represented one of my brief but active encounters with Middle East royalty.

Unlike what I expected, the prince conducted himself like an ordinary citizen. I detected nothing condescending about him, nor did I ever feel uncomfortable around him. He spoke English very well, readily engaged in humor and made me, at least, feel very comfortable. It was a pleasure to be in his company.

Dr. Green had, and I am sure still has, a gift for writing as well as editing. She successfully served as ghostwriter for several prominent Hollywood personalities and coached students from several Southern California institutions in writing their academic papers. When the students were unable to produce what she considered acceptable academic treatises, she would sometimes rewrite the papers or request that the students rewrite them. The results were almost always outstanding, and the acceptable documents were produced in a reasonably short period of time.

As the months passed and we began to work more closely together, I sensed substantial differences in operational and management styles. Where I was more a consensus builder and team player, Dr. Green often preferred to make independent decisions and communicate them to her coworkers. Our different styles tended to result in conflict and/or misunderstanding.

Dr. Green greatly enjoyed the Hollywood scene but regularly contended that to become an influential person in the entertainment world one either had to be

Jewish or remain friendly with Jewish people. How true that contention is remains to be determined.

Dr. Green herself had a Jewish background. She often lamented that her discoveries regarding the lost continent Atlantis had been suppressed by the Jewish people and the Catholics. Both groups, in her opinion, thought the discovery of the continent would contradict the teachings of the Bible.

She was of medium height with an attractive face. Her blonde-gray hair distinguished her from other ladies her age. Dr. Green's interest and belief in tarot cards, horoscopes and fortunetelling were strong and important to her decision-making. Once on a trip to New Orleans, Louisiana, she could hardly wait to enter the open-air market to have her fortune read. She had heard that the lady reading the tarot cards very often proved accurate in her predictions and she wanted to get the lady's reading on her stay in New Orleans so she would know what to plan for and how to arrange her time there.

Our often-conflicting management styles prompted me to withdraw gradually to the sidelines and leave the decisions to Dr. Green. I continued to work with her for some time from a distance but established a school known as Nobel University, headquartered in the U.S. Virgin Islands, and an association intended to review and promote worthy institutions outside the United States known as the Global Education Association. I intended to have the school serve students outside the United States and had every intention of developing standards that would be acceptable to most academicians. The Global Education Association never became very active.

I gradually withdrew from all the activities I had undertaken with Dr. Green and severed my relationship with her and her businesses. Because of our different operational styles, I could not see the possibility of evolving the type of organization I had had in mind when we joined forces.

I never really talked with Dr. Green after withdrawing from her operation, and I never got the impression that my withdrawal made any difference to her. She never seemed to act on sentiment but on what she saw as reality that favored her advancement, at least as she interpreted advancement. She, however, continued to use my name online until I requested that it be removed from her web site. She readily complied with my request for which I was very grateful.

Online references indicate that Dr. Green continues to operate an online university and an accrediting agency. Dr. Green's operations seemed revolutionary when established and appeared to have outstanding potential. Few online courses were offered in the early 1990s, and busy individuals from around the world were eager for alternative methods of delivery.

My attempts at unaccredited certificate programs through Nobel University and the global accreditation of institutions proved fruitless and detrimental to my professional reputation. I still believe a global accrediting agency is needed but I'm not willing to risk my future on the establishment of such an organization. I doubt that Dr. Green's efforts can ever be accepted among traditional academicians.

Under the right conditions, I believe the concepts Dr. Green and I introduced in the early 1990s could have presented positive, student-beneficial challenges to the then- rigid educational establishment. With the advantage of hindsight, I believe both of us were over-zealous in our efforts to get something underway without adequate preparation.

DegreeInfo continues to view Dr. Green and her organizations almost as illegal institutions worthy of nothing but criticism and defamation. Perhaps much of the criticism is warranted. Certainly, the sale of degrees is not professionally acceptable. But, conceptually Dr. Green pushed the envelope of   distance learning. Today, more and more traditional institutions are offering online options. This burgeoning group of online classes calls for changes in the approach to accreditation.

Chapter 20

>>>>))((((<<

My Tenure at Notre Dame de Namur University

After leaving Armstrong University in the early 1990s, I began teaching at the fifth oldest institution of higher education in California: College of Notre Dame. The college was in good standing with the Western Association of Schools and Colleges and enjoyed a stellar reputation. It had been founded by the Sisters of Notre Dame in 1851 and chartered in 1868 as the first college in the State of California to offer the baccalaureate degree to women. The student enrollment was between 1,000 and 1,500 when I began my tenure at the college.

Initially, I taught one class, then two. After two years, I was asked to be a full-time instructor. I readily agreed. The students had very open minds and were extremely respectful. They particularly enjoyed discussions focusing on customs and the conduct of business throughout the Middle East and Asia. I enjoyed working with them and cooperating with the faculty. Ultimately, I accepted the chairmanship of the MBA Program, thereby entering once again into academic administration.

Dr. Smith, the college president who served during my first few years as a full-time employee at

Notre Dame, was open to new ideas and experimentation and championed growth and outreach. And so, with her permission and blessing, I began to reach out to the community. As Chairman of the MBA Program, I gathered an impressive group of executives from well-known Silicon-Valley firms and formed an active Board of Advisors. The Board helped introduce the MBA Program to the Peninsula business community and actively raised funds.

The growth of the MBA Program and the success of the MBA Board of Advisors in reaching out to the community awakened in me a strong desire to see the other business programs grow and prosper. I could see a bright future for an integrated School of Business, and I began talking with the president about forming such a school, thereby bringing the disparate programs into one academic unit. The president responded positively, but early in the formation process she either decided to move on or was asked to do so. The one thing she did promise was that she would see that the Board of Directors approved the school formation before her departure. She fulfilled her promise, and the School of Business and Management was formed in 2001. Shortly after the School's formation, I agreed to serve as Acting Dean.

The formation of the School of Business and Management seemed to awaken an interest throughout the college in integrating diverse programs into schools. Soon after the business school emerged, several other schools developed: the School of Arts and Humanities; the School of Sciences; and, the School of Education and Leadership.

Most of the college faculty seemed pleased with the school structure, but some faculty members preferred the departmental-program arrangement. One faculty member in particular would comment each time he saw me, "You're the cause of all this change. Why didn't you leave things as they were?"

The gentleman who replaced Dr. Smith showed less enthusiasm for my efforts at expanding and improving the School of Business than had Dr. Smith; despite the apparent lack of enthusiasm, I continued to promote the school in the immediate community and beyond. The School of Business sponsored and organized a well-attended Distinguished Speakers Series and attracted groups of international business people and professors. One group of Japanese businessmen, for example, presented a panel discussion on the basics of organizational behavior to the students enrolled in the college's Organizational Behavior class. A group of Japanese professors held a two-day seminar at the college in which Notre Dame's Graduate Dean and other college administrators participated. The college's name and the name of the School of Business began to circulate not only throughout Silicon Valley but internationally as well.

The Distinguished Speakers Series and many of the seminars were conducted in the beautiful Ralston

Hall on the college campus. The hall enjoys the status of a California Registered Landmark and a National Historic Landmark. It served originally as the home of William Chapman Ralston, founder of the Bank of California. The Sisters of Notre Dame purchased the Ralston estate and made the hall the focus of the college campus. It seems potential seismic difficulties have recently emerged, requiring extensive repairs to the beautiful building. I trust and hope the finances for the refurbishing of the hall are forthcoming.

Soon after the formation of the Board of Advisors, we began to seek out potential donors first for the MBA Program and later for the School of Business. Through the Board's efforts and the members' support of my attempt at fundraising, the program and later the School were able to raise sufficient funds for the Distinguished Speakers Series and the various seminars. Further, the program as well as the school received donations for projects designed to further enhance the various activities.

Shortly after assuming office, Dr. Smith's replacement skillfully maneuvered a change of name for the institution from College of Notre Dame to Notre Dame de Namur University. The response to the name change was generally positive, but, interestingly, a man who listed himself as a "Senior Member" of Degree-Info, posted the following comment on the Degree-Info.com website:

"Another head-scratching name change: Notre Dame de Namur University" The College of Notre Dame, here in Northern California, has been doing a fine job for 150+ years. But when they felt the stirrings to advertise themselves, they could not go for "Notre Dame University," since some guys in Indiana did that. So they took the full name of the order that founded them, and, as of a couple of weeks ago, are known as Notre Dame de Namur University. Thus they may have become the only American school with two words of ambiguous pronunciation in their name, if we don't count the real (but secret) name of DQ University." (www.degreeinfo.com/off-topic-discussions/3510-another-head-scratching-name)

The comment may have been made in jest, but it hardly seems appropriate to compare, even in a facetious fashion, Notre Dame de Namur University to D-Q University, the actual name of which was De-ganawidah-Quetzalcoatl University. D-Q had just lost its accreditation and was in the process of closing its doors as an institution of higher education.

After noticing the inroads the School of Business was making in the community and the funds the

Board of Advisors and I were raising, the Vice President for Development of the university asked me if I would cooperate with his office in fundraising and the introduction of the university to major corporations. I accepted the vice president's invitation to work part-time with him. I began my work in the development office thinking that the vice president and chancellor had at least discussed the matter. Some months later, however, I discovered the two had not talked about sharing my services, and despite putting the vice president in touch with various wealthy and influential executives and opening doors for potential donations, I was severely criticized by the chancellor and told not to do any development work. Raising funds and introducing potential benefactors to the university were considered a conflict of interest rather than a contribution to the advancement of the university.

When Dr. Smith resigned, I submitted my application for the presidency. I thought I definitely had the academic as well as the diplomatic and administrative experience to function effectively as the chief executive officer of a small institution. After all, I had already served for some three years in such a capacity. I consulted with Mahin, who admonished me not to apply, but I foolishly didn't listen.

"Mahin, Dr. Smith has resigned the presidency and I would like to apply for the job. I have the qualifications," I stated one morning.

Mahin at first didn't respond to my comment but after a minute or two answered, "Frank, you are making a mistake. Your application will not be accepted, and you are placing yourself in a difficult situation if the application is rejected."

"Why should the application make any difference?" I asked.

"Whoever the new president is, he or she will not trust you but will think you are against him or her," Mahin said.

My application was rejected but was, I am sure, made known to the new president and the chancellor. I still feel I could have made a major contribution to the further development of the university. Mahin was probably right. I never felt Dr. Smith's replacement trusted or even liked me.

My attempt to integrate the new president into my development efforts for the School of Business and create the possibility of expanding those efforts through him to the institution itself proved impossible, much to my detriment. I invited him to accompany me on a visit with the vice-president of a major technology company. Both the vice-president and I had served in Iran and had several acquaintances in common. We discussed Iranian politics and the possible future of the country. As soon as we left the meeting, the president asked me, "How long did you work for the C.I.A.?"

"I never joined the Agency," I replied. "As the General Manager of the U.S. Chamber of Commerce in Tehran, I interacted with a large number of U.S. and Iranian business people as did the vice president."

No explanation of my activities in Iran seemed to dissuade the president from his impression that I had served as an American spy in the Middle East for several years prior to the Islamic Revolution.

In the late 1990s, the university began discussing the need for a new dormitory. Donations for the construction of the dormitory were not forthcoming, and I happened to discover two potential investors interested in financing the venture. The potential investors made a sincere proposal to the administration, but the proposal was rejected outright. The university as well as the potential investors could have benefitted greatly, but circumstances did not seem to permit the development of an appropriate business venture. I understand the proposed dormitory was not constructed until 2005.

Despite my many contributions to the university, I faced an academic trial one Monday morning. I arrived at the office around 9 a.m. and settled in for what I thought would be a fruitful work week. That mid-morning, I received a telephone call asking me to go at once to the president's office. The caller gave no hint as to the reason for the call.

Upon entering the office, I was immediately accused of unethical operations that would lessen the prestige of the university. Nobel University and my attempt at establishing a global accrediting agency seemed anathema to the president and the group present in the room. One individual outside the university suggested that the activities might have been too entrepreneurial for the average academic institution. Whatever the case, Nobel University and the proposed accrediting agency did not meet with approval from the university administration.

The jury I faced consisted of the president, the chancellor and two other members of the university staff. There was, however, no one in attendance who could defend me or help me explain the rationale for my activities, and I was too shocked to effectively defend myself. At the end of the short trial, I was told to clear out my office, go home and wait for further instructions.

When I returned to my office, I felt I was in foreign territory. I could hardly enter the room that I had become accustomed to, nor could I focus on anything. My head was abuzz; my heart was pumping.

I hurriedly cleared the office and drove home unnerved and depressed. I felt I had successfully served as a stabilizing force for the formation and efficient operation of the School of Business. The structure of the business area prior to the formation of the school had been chaotic, at best, and I knew I could find areas where the school could lower its costs while continuing to develop. I was certain that I could stimulate new growth for the school through my contacts and those of the Board of Advisors. I soon decided, however, that the fight to keep my position at the university would not be worthwhile.

The day following the trial, I was told not to return to my office or assume any of my duties as Interim Dean until a decision regarding my status had been made. I hibernated in our recently purchased condominium for three days but did get in touch with one member of my Board of Advisors as well as one of my associates and travel partners from San Francisco State University. Both gentlemen advised me to consult with an attorney and perhaps engage his/her services in my defense.

A local attorney accepted my case and began discussions with the university. He encouraged me to sue the university because he felt I had a good case against it, but I declined the opportunity. I didn't want to bring any negative attention to the institution, nor did I want to create more animosity toward me than already existed. After all, the conflict and bitterness did not actually involve the university or the majority of its staff. My difficulties were with a select group of powerful individuals within the institution's administrative structure.

Negotiations with the university continued for several weeks before a final agreement was reached. That agreement prohibited me from ever setting foot on the campus again or participating in any event there. The agreement also called for my resignation, which I submitted without delay. A letter was placed in my file for an indefinite period of time.

More than twelve years have passed since my unfortunate conflict with the institution's elite, and a new administration has emerged. I have abided by the agreement and have not entered the campus even when invited by outside groups or former associates to do so. I regret that the university did not allow me more freedom for entrepreneurial activities but can understand the restraints under which it operated and, in all probability, continues to operate.

I felt I was a vital part of the institution for several years and enjoyed my tenure there and the association with its employees. Immediately following my resignation, I harbored resentment and even a bit of hatred toward those individuals I considered responsible for my departure, but as the years have passed, I have been able to forgive while not forgetting. I admire the current president's strong code of ethics and know that the university is in good hands. My only regret is that I have not been able to make the contribution to the advancement of the institution that I know I could have made and would have loved to have made.

Shortly after my resignation, Mahin and I decided to sell the beautifully-situated condominium we had purchased approximately one year before and return to Walnut Creek. We disposed of the condominium within a matter of weeks and were off to a new adventure.

Each time I recall my tenure at Notre Dame de Namur University, I think of the sentence that the founder of the institution apparently loved and quoted on a variety of occasions: "How good is the good God." That sentence speaks volumes, and I feel certain it applies to both the institution and me. God has certainly been good to me and I am certain He has been and will continue to be good to the university. Despite a disappointing end to what I believe to have been a very successful tenure at the institution, I refused to retreat into my virtual Pepper Tree Kingdom.

Chapter 21

>>>>>)(<<<<<

A Lesson in Church Politics

It all began with a midday telephone call early in 2001 from Dr. John Westfall, the Senior Pastor of Walnut Creek Presbyterian Church and former Lecturer in the School of Business at Notre Dame de Namur University. Dr. Westfall inquired whether or not I would be interested in applying for the position of Business Manager of the church. The Business Manager of several years had moved on, and Dr. Westfall wanted to replace the Interim Manager with a regular employee.

"I know you're not at the university now and am wondering if you might consider applying for the Business Manager position that is open at the church," Dr. Westfall said.

"I will need to talk with Mahin about the possibility," I responded as casually as I could. "Can I have a few days to think about the offer and get back to you?"

"No problem," Dr. Westfall responded. "But I would like to have an answer as soon as possible."

We ended the brief conversation with my promise to let him know within two or three days.

The possibility of working for a church not only intrigued me, but seemed to answer a short prayer I had quietly repeated almost daily since my departure from Notre Dame de Namur.

"God, I feel you want me to serve you in some way. Please show me Your will, and I will do my best to comply with Your command."

I viewed the call from Dr. Westfall as a direct message from God and a possible opportunity to serve His Kingdom.

The day following Dr. Westfall's telephone call, I informed Mahin of the offer and asked what she thought about it.

"You know Dr. Westfall and seem to like him very much, but accepting a job in Walnut Creek will require another move for us." We were living in San Mateo at the time.

"Don't worry about the necessary move," Mahin encouraged. "Perhaps working at a church will be good for your morale. You need to do something uplifting after your experience at the university."

I immediately informed Dr. Westfall that I was interested in the job, and within two weeks I was interviewed, first by the Personnel Elders and two evenings later by the Finance Elders. The interviews were cordial but thorough. Around ten days after the interviews, I was offered the position.

I was eager to work with Dr. Westfall. His sermons and teaching always seemed genuine and intriguing, and when I accepted the Interim Deanship at Notre Dame de Namur University, I aimed to develop a new course for which I thought his talents were appropriate. When he agreed to develop and co-teach a class entitled "The Moral Character of Business," I was delighted and made immediate arrangements for him to begin the course development and lectures. Making those arrangements enabled me to talk frequently with Dr. Westfall and I became increasingly fond of him. His success with the students dispelled any questions anyone might have had concerning his teaching capabilities.

I asked for and was granted a two-week grace period before assuming my duties so that Mahin and I could settle in temporary quarters in Rossmoor, the huge compound for adults over the age of fifty-five in Walnut Creek. I excitedly began my work within the agreed-upon time frame.

WCPC's history extended back more than one hundred years. The church was established in the late 19th century in downtown Walnut Creek on Locust Avenue but later moved to its current location after a larger building had been completed to accommodate the increased attendance. A major fire destroyed the sanctuary in the early 1980s, and a new sanctuary was designed and built later in the decade.

My first four years at WCPC proved very enjoyable and, in my opinion, productive. I always had access to Dr. Westfall's office and could bring up almost anything related to the church for discussion. During those four years, the church furthered its reputation as a caring organization, willing to actively participate in civic affairs. The non-profit housing group known as Satellite Housing and the church cooperated in the construction of a subsidized housing unit behind the sanctuary and successfully addressed what had long been a drainage problem on church property. A dedicated church member conceived and established a training program for disabled individuals capable only of performing such menial tasks as vacuuming floors and washing windows. In conjunction with the Red Cross and St. Paul's Episcopal Church on Trinity Avenue, WCPC began the process of identifying itself as an emergency shelter.

Gradually, however, the mood within a minor segment of the church membership became increasingly negative and belligerent. In 2005, the ill feelings of certain individuals eventually surfaced in a challenge to Dr. Westfall's leadership. Members of the unhappy segment persuaded church leaders to call a special meeting at which several individuals asked for Dr. Westfall's resignation. His resignation from the pastorate occurred several months later. Thus began over eighteen months without adequate pastoral leadership.

I didn't believe at first that the opposition to Dr. Westfall would be successful. He always seemed open to new ideas and dialogue; he certainly preached well. I gradually realized that his inability to relate to older members of the church cost him his pastorate.

Dr. Westfall's resignation depressed both Mahin and me. I can recall one occasion when I found Mahin crying in our bedroom.

"I miss John," Mahin said, referring to Dr. Westfall by his first name. "He was such a good friend and so easy to talk with."

"I miss him, too. He was an inspiration and a counselor. But he's gone, and we need to adjust."

"Eventually, I will be able to accept the fact that he is no longer around," Mahin muttered. "But it won't be easy."

From WCPC, Dr. Westfall moved to Edina, Minnesota, a small city near Minneapolis, where he assumed the pastorate of a Congregational Church known as the Colonial Church of Edina. He knew the move was a risk but decided the risk was more desirable than playing it safe.

According to his online biography, Dr. Westfall felt he could help the church reverse its ten years of decline and put it on an upward trajectory. He assumed the congregation was ready to initiate new strategies and approaches to ministry, but his assumption proved incorrect. In fewer than two years he found himself back in Seattle, where he had served at University Presbyterian Church for a number of years.

Since returning to Seattle, Dr. Westfall has planted a church known as The Harbor Church. He trusts and hopes that the church can attract people in an area famous for its low-church attendance.

Dr. Westfall's resignation left quite a void at WCPC, particularly as related to the staff. The interim pastor proved to be an acceptable speaker but unwilling to devote more than ten to twelve hours per week to pastoral duties. Because of my attempts to speak up and offer my opinion concerning certain administrative topics, he forbade me to attend staff meetings and, for all practical purposes, made me persona non grata for most of his time at the church.

Nor did I receive a word of thanks or recognition from any church authorities. They themselves were operating under very trying circumstances. I performed my duties out of love for God, the church and the congregants. I needed no praise but did at times long for understanding and acceptance. I began to question the validity of my spiritual journey and love for the church.

During the period between senior pastors, the church had no focus, nor did it have any expressed formal or informal rules. After approximately one year of inadequate pastoral leadership, the Session, the governing body of local Presbyterian churches, agreed it was time to set up a search committee for a new senior pastor. The committee was formed, and the search began.

Several months passed before any announcement was made regarding the progress of the search.

The church suffered from a reputation for being hard on its pastors. Some of Dr. Westfall's predecessors apparently ended their tenure in a fashion similar to Dr. Westfall's. Other pastors had found it difficult, if not impossible, to unify the church and reduce the conflict among opposing groups of members.

Members of former search committees confided to me that several times in the past search committee members who approached potential pastoral candidates had been told by a number of the candidates that they were not willing to subject themselves to the treatment they associated with WCPC. They preferred to remain where they were or pursue other pastoral possibilities.

After approximately one year, the chair of the search committee made public the name of a promising pastoral candidate, Reverend James Fallow, and announced a date he and his family would visit Walnut Creek from San Juan Capistrano, California. At the request of the committee, I arranged a dinner for several prominent church officials at a local restaurant so they could meet the candidate and interact with him and his wife on an informal basis. The dinner appeared to be a success.

Reverend Fallow was offered the pastorate and accepted it without delay. Some gossip regarding his departure from his previous pastorate surfaced, but it remained in the realm of hearsay. The precise reason for the departure was never fully revealed publicly.

Whatever the real cause of resignation from the pastorate in Southern California, WCPC needed to welcome its new senior pastor with graciousness and without speculating on his past or focusing on WCPC's past.

I personally welcomed the new pastor. I had great hopes of being able to work with him and further WCPC's mission both locally and internationally. My primary purpose was to serve God by supporting the new pastor and making certain that he succeeded. I had no other intentions in relation to the church.

Initially, Reverend Fallow seemed eager to have me work with him. He talked about meetings I should attend as Business Manager and hinted at an extension of my duties and authority. In response to what I perceived as an interest in evolving a working relationship, I made every attempt to serve and please him. I even developed and presented him with a detailed communication plan and suggestions for what I considered to be an appropriate administrative structure. The plan and suggestions were based on my more than seven years as Business Manager.

I waited for a response to my suggested plan and structure but never received one. The lack of response puzzled me. If the pastor hadn't liked the suggested plan and structure, I would have expected him to tell me they were not what he wanted and perhaps provide guidance in the development of a communication plan and administrative structure with which he would have felt comfortable. Gradually, I was able to rationalize the lack of response as not a snub to me but as a need on his part to get into the pastoral routine more before focusing on the improvement of communication or making administrative changes.

As I continued to watch Mr. Fallow, who later became Dr. Fallow, function and perform his duties, I began to worry. Even though he appeared very eager to shepherd the congregation, he showed a certain naiveté and fear of people. He seemed to have relatively little self-confidence. He seemed a strong candidate for subjugation by a domineering person. Of course, such a person was nearby and began to endear herself to him. That person had long wanted to be my nemesis at the church and now saw the opportunity to do so.

I labored for some fourteen months under Pastor Fallow, making every effort to communicate and work out a modus operandi, but gradually I realized I wasn't making any headway and decided to invite him out to lunch and attempt to discover what I needed to do to gain his confidence. The lunch did not, however, serve the purpose for which it was intended. Midway through the lunch, Mr. Fallow informed me that I wouldn't continue to serve much longer as business manager. He said he had hoped to tell me of my dismissal in a more delicate manner and under different circumstances, but since I had brought up the subject of working more closely with him, he felt it was prudent to let me know immediately of his plans, which did not include me.

After a few weeks, the personnel committee of the church announced a date for interviews for my position. I subconsciously understood my time at the church was very limited, but had a great deal of difficulty rationalizing the sudden turn of events. I foolishly applied for the job.

The day of my interview arrived, and I appeared before the members of the committee. When I entered the room, I immediately felt I wouldn't be judged fairly or given an unbiased opportunity to present my case.

"We apologize for being a little unorganized," one committee member stated. "But I'm sure you realize we have been very busy. Shall we begin the interview?"

What could I say? Neither the timeframe nor the content of the interview was in my hands. All I could say was, "I'm ready when you are."

Rather than the Chair of the Personnel Committee being in charge of the interview, my nemesis, the person who had attempted to bias and had apparently succeeded in turning the new pastor against me, was in charge. My heart sank, and I merely went through the interview routine. I had to acknowledge immediately that the playing field wasn't level and that I should be prepared to receive a rejection.

"We hope to make our decision soon and will let you know the outcome of the interviews within the next few days," my nemesis articulated.

Feeling deflated, I managed to muster up a "Thank you," and immediately left the room.

The formal rejection came within a few days. What a charade the entire interview process had proved to be. I whipped myself psychologically for even entertaining the thought that I might be able to persuade the committee that I was still a capable person.

I was, therefore, at least somewhat prepared for my termination but was still taken aback by the abrupt way in which the dismissal was executed. When the Chair of the Personnel Committee and her associate entered the room, they hardly acknowledged my presence.

"Today is your last day of employment," they merely stated. "You may empty your office before the end of the working day."

No recognition of my accomplishments as business manager or a goodbye reception was mentioned. They obviously wanted me out immediately. My last day on the job was in September 2009.

Immediately, I gathered my belongings and closed my files. Throughout the process of preparing to vacate the office, I told myself not to be depressed. I repeatedly stressed to myself that I had done nothing wrong and shouldn't feel rejected. The manner in which I had been dismissed, however, did weigh heavily on me. It tended to make me bitter and caused me to question the concepts of Christian charity and brotherly love.

Added to the disappointing pattern of behavior by the personnel committee chair and her cohort, was the surprising failure of Reverend Fallow to appear. Throughout the afternoon, I kept thinking that he would at least come to the door of my office to bid me goodbye, but he didn't appear. He apparently remained in his office until after I left the building. I was surprised at the lack of cordiality, but I shouldn't have been. He treated me the same way he had treated other departing employees—ignoring me and not offering even one word of thank you. This unfortunate behavior on the last day of my employment at the church hurt me terribly, and it was not until after two years that the senior pastor and I were able to meet twice at a neutral location and discuss that last day. Those meetings helped me overcome some of my bitterness and forgive all three of the individuals involved in my dismissal.

Although it was never discussed openly, several church members have told me that the decision to replace me as business manager resulted, at least in part, from my close association with Dr. Westfall. These members have said I was considered "his boy," loyal primarily to him rather than to the church. Nothing could have been further from the truth.

Granted, I had worked with Dr. Westfall for almost four years and greatly respected him. I could not really understand the insistence of the group in ridding the congregation of an individual who had their best interests at heart. Perhaps he didn't fit their mold. Perhaps I hadn't fit the mold either. But my ultimate loyalty was to the Christian faith, WCPC and its mission.

My dedication to Christianity and the church had existed since early childhood. Dad had been a Pentecostal preacher and much too legalistic for me, but his influence on my life vis-à-vis spiritual interests and pursuits had been significant. While an undergraduate, I had served in a tiny Pentecostal church in Wilmington, California, as a teaching pastor, having been ordained and admitted to the membership of a small organization known as The Associated Brotherhood of Christians. The pastor of the church was Reverend E. E. Partridge, one of the two ministers who had worked diligently to found the group in the 1930s and incorporate it during World War II.

I worked with Reverend Partridge for approximately three years during the early 1960s. Unlike Dad, he was open-minded and quite willing to listen, reason and encourage younger people even if their ideas did not agree with his. I thoroughly enjoyed working with Reverent Partridge and gained substantially from his wisdom.

Following my three years as teaching pastor, I didn't renew my license with the Associated Brotherhood of Christians. Instead, I pursued a bachelor's degree in Religious Science, which, at the time, intrigued me. I began but did not complete work toward a master's degree in the same field.

While living in Iran and Saudi Arabia, I had a strong interest in Islam and Islamic culture and toyed with the idea of converting to Islam. The history of the Islamic movements, both the Sunni and the Shia, intrigued me but my background and faith in Christianity prevailed. Although I didn't convert to Islam, I developed a deep respect for the religion and non-fanatical Moslems. Religious faith and spirituality remained extremely important to me whatever the religion.

My devotion to God and His Kingdom inspire me to serve a church and its ordained shepherds fervently. Like Asaph in Psalm 73, I desire nothing more than to be close to God and feel serving the church helps me draw closer to Him. I dislike displays of piety but greatly respect quiet reverence expressed in deed and action.

Sometimes it seems my closeness to God almost slips from me and I nearly lose my foothold. But then some event or development like a small bird flying over my head chirping a message of love and compassion reawakens my trust in God. I realize God permeates both heaven and earth, and I reaffirm my belief that He desires my love as much as I long to be in fellowship with Him. The spiritual world offers something to me the material world cannot provide and I continue searching for the grace that purifies me despite my shortcomings.

In my opinion, no church should emphasize categories into which individuals are made to fit but should concentrate on sharing the gospel and offering fellowship to all who seek it. It is to serve as a beacon in the community, show kindness and compassion and "look after orphans and widows." (James 1:27) It should be an institution dedicated to serving the needs of all mankind.

The phrase "church politics" refers to the ways church leaders relate to each other, the staff and church members in exercising authority and deciding how things will be done in church. Too often, as my own situation at WCPC clearly demonstrated, the politics are negative, without the love that Jesus taught. Too often those church leaders who profess dedication to Christian ideals and Christ-like behavior labor under the burden of huge egos and forget their commission of incorporating the church into the life of the community and serving mankind regardless of religious affiliation or economic standing.

Rather than even thinking of permanently retreating into my virtual Pepper Tree Kingdom to avoid the un-Christian-like ways that so often characterize interaction within the church, I have pledged to myself to continue my walk with God and seek His guidance for my future. I continue to make every effort to accept His will in spite of how circumstances may appear at a particular time, and with even greater vigor I strive for the fullness of the image of God in my soul.

Chapter 22

The Die Is Cast

The day was sunny and beautiful. I had worked hard during the morning so that I could take my two oldest grandsons, Dominic and Isaac, to the movies and allow Mahin to catch up on her chores at home. I made certain everything was in order prior to my departure for the day; I was eager for noon to arrive because I knew I would enjoy the afternoon with the two boys.

At noon sharp, I said goodbye to my co-workers and headed for home. The car seemed to run more smoothly than usual, and the brilliant sun that reflected off the hood of the Camry might have blinded me had I not been wearing dark glasses.

Driving down Ygnacio Valley Road, I looked up at Mount Diablo and the brown hills not far from Walnut Creek, California. The greenery from the spring rains had been rendered brown by the summer heat, and the soil was obviously quite dry. I knew it wouldn't rain this time of the year. The heat was the norm. The sun was destined to shine at least until October or November.

No thought of sickness or death entered my mind as I drove onto the short street where our townhouse was located. Only thoughts of fun, relaxation and getting to know my grandsons better occupied my mind. Both Mahin and I seemed to be in good health. We had at least a few more years together to enjoy our daughters, our grandchildren and each other.

The street was quiet and nearly deserted. I could hear voices from the nearby swimming pool but couldn't see the swimmers. The voices sounded joyful and relaxed. Many of the families in the complex known as Bancroft Village were savoring their mid-summer vacations, taking advantage of the weather by sun bathing or swimming. The entire ambiance height-ened my anticipation.

As I entered our townhouse, I saw our two grandsons sitting in the living room. I called Mahin's name but got no response. I walked into the living room and asked the boys where their grandmother was. They first looked at each other and then pointed to my office. They seemed hesitant to say anything but finally told me that Mahin had been sleeping for more than an hour. She hadn't completed the preparation of their lunch before she went into the office and fell asleep.

I quickly checked the office and found Mahin slumped in the chair in front of my desk. She looked as if she were sleeping, but she was making a peculiar sound as she breathed. I stopped for a minute, think-ing she was simply tired and needed a rest. After all, we had been very busy for several days.

I touched her, but she didn't respond. Suddenly, something registered with me. Mahin was not sleeping. And she was not moving. She obviously was not well. I feared the worst. I needed to get help. *My God. Is she going to die? Has she had a stroke? No.*

I tried to reassure myself that everything would be fine.

She will be all right. I will call 911. Certainly, the emergency crew can revive her and make sure she is all right.

Long-term hospitalization or death wasn't possible at that time. We had too many positive things to look forward to.

I literally leaped into the kitchen and dialed the number I had often heard about but had never used. I was still confident that Mahin would be all right but wanted to make certain she received the appropriate care without delay. My two grandsons sat stone still. I am certain they understood that I was worried, but, like me, they probably didn't grasp the gravity of the situation.

Mahin had endured chemotherapy and surgery for breast cancer some fifteen years earlier and had also been diagnosed with a minor heart problem, but neither of these conditions seemed to worry her or prevent her from maintaining a busy schedule. In fact, the doctor had indicated just a few weeks before that her health was fairly good. She had a threshold for pain that I didn't have and seldom complained about any ailment. She accepted what came her way and seemed to relax more and more as the years passed.

While the emergency crew was on its way, I happened to recall a particular incident that had occurred during her bout with cancer; that recollection gave me some courage. We were on our afternoon walk along a local trail when Mahin suddenly declared she had to lie down. That was all she said as she spread herself out on the asphalt. Her statement and action frightened me, and I quizzed her as to the reason for her sudden tiredness.

"Oh," she said. "It's nothing. The hormone shots have just gotten to me."

That was all she said, and after a few minutes, she got up. We completed our walk without another reference to the cancer or her need to rest. Recollection of that incident was soothing to my nerves.

Much of our free time was spent with friends, walking and trying to keep in shape. Mahin was always interested in reducing her weight and viewed exercise not only as a means for weight loss but also as a way to keep as fit as possible. Even when she didn't really feel like exercising or didn't feel well, she attempted to keep active. She suffered considerably from the cancer and initially from the fear of a heart attack, but her determination seemed to overcome any health difficulty she had or might have. I felt a great deal of respect for her determination not to succumb to any illness or threat of sickness. I hoped that if I were ever ill, I could be as brave and positive as she was.

Within minutes, the emergency team arrived, examined Mahin and declared that she would have to be transported to the local hospital as soon as possible. They only said her situation was serious but gave me no further information. I could ride in the ambulance or follow in my own car. I opted to follow in the car.

I knew four of my immediate neighbors well and understood that they were aware of the arrival of the ambulance. There was not much they could do, however. They could only wait with me to see what developed.

I called our daughter Ladan, Dominic and Isaac's mother, and explained the situation as clearly as I possibly could. Ladan told me she would arrange to have the two boys picked up so that I wouldn't have the responsibility of taking care of them under the uncertain circumstances. Two young gentlemen from WCPC where I was employed agreed to stay with the grandsons until they were picked up later that day.

During the five to ten minutes it took me to arrive at the hospital, I realized a crisis had hit me. I thought I was responding calmly and with a clear mind. I was even conceiving a plan for what I would do and how I would do it while Mahin was in the hospital. I was not aware that an aneurysm had burst. The seriousness of her condition had not yet become a reality for me. I was facing something bigger than I knew.

I drove to the hospital in a daze. I had the valet park my car and rushed to the floor where they had taken Mahin. Upon my arrival, I was told to sit in the waiting room. There was nothing I could do but wait. Unaccustomed to waiting for a diagnosis for someone so dear to me, I became agitated. My body felt strained and tense.

I was strangely fascinated and overwhelmed by the moment—fascinated by the development and overwhelmed by its seriousness and unpredictability. Even though I tended to retreat into my virtual Pepper Tree Kingdom and my physical appearance never showed much strength, I was strong emotionally. My inability to interact in a crowd may have encouraged onlookers to think of me as an emotional weakling.

The word about Mahin's condition spread quickly, and friends and neighbors began to appear in the waiting room of the hospital. Almost everyone present tried to console, support and encourage me. They also showed considerable concern for Mahin's elderly sister, Esmat, who finally made her way to the waiting room with her walker. Even though we all hoped for the best and feigned a positive attitude, we appeared like a large, distraught family.

I tried desperately to maintain my composure but made few comments except to greet the visitors and attempt light conversation. Several individuals in the room tried unsuccessfully to engage me, but the tone remained heavy and uncertain. Suddenly, it dawned on me that I might lose the love of my life.

As the sadness and stress took over my body and mind, I began to think about my childhood, the California pepper tree near the cottage where my grandmother had lived and my tendency to retreat literally or figuratively into my imaginary Pepper Tree Kingdom under that tree where I could withdraw and pursue my identity search in complete privacy. Would I retreat permanently into my imaginary kingdom if Mahin passed on? Suddenly, I wasn't sure who I was, a person who would revert to the quandary that had plagued me much of my earlier life or a liberated being capable of going forward without my life partner? Would I or could I be the same person without Mahin, or would I isolate myself to avoid interaction with others? I couldn't answer those questions at that moment, but I began to worry about both Mahin and myself.

Gradually, I grasped the extreme need I had to understand myself and know who I was and would become, particularly if Mahin died. Psychologically, I suddenly surrendered like a cut blossom on a hot day. I didn't sob aloud but did cry inwardly. I had to cry to avoid the emotional abyss I felt myself sliding into. Why did Mahin have to become ill now? I loved her so much, and she was my support system—my world, my everything. Could she continue to support me in spirit while not being physically present?

I knew I could have used help, but because of my long years of psychological isolation, except with Mahin, I couldn't bring myself to cry out for assistance. I couldn't show weakness. I didn't want those people around me to know how I felt, nor did I want to inconvenience them with my burden. Many of the friends probably would have welcomed the opportunity to contribute to my psychological well being; I couldn't see that possibility at the time. How could they grasp my preoccupation with my identity without knowing my history? And I was in no mood to discuss that part of my life with anyone.

Mahin was on life support for about forty-eight hours, but then our daughters and I decided to remove her from life support. The doctors informed me that it might be best for Mahin to succumb to her attack. If she lived, she would remain in a vegetative state. The ruptured aneurism had completely destroyed her brain. Her death was preferred to a vegetative stage for life.

She died fewer than twenty-four hours after she was removed from life-support. I knew she wouldn't want me to revert to my old ways of avoiding a challenge and retreating into my virtual Pepper Tree Kingdom. Thus, my identity search started anew and continues to this day in her honor. My beloved wife, I'm sure, still watches over me, still wishes the best for me.

She was and still is, the best gift that God has bestowed on me.

Chapter 23

>>>))(((<<<

My Gradual Epiphany

I have spent a major portion of my life searching for my identity and often reinventing myself to meet the particular expectations of the group with whom I have been working or associating. My "self" at any point in time has been an effort on my part to be someone every person or at least the majority of people could trust and admire. My own opinions have often been hidden to accommodate the group and its views. I have often attempted to trust and have placed my trust in persons I should have avoided. Not knowing how or when to trust leaves a person open to misuse by others and further withdrawal from reality into the protection of a figurative low-hanging California pepper tree.

Unlike the New Testament apostle Paul (Saul), I did not have a blinding flash of understanding regarding my identity but have experienced a gradual realization that life is a gift and I need to live it to the fullest. Slowly, I have accepted the reality that my identity is not dependent upon a specific individual or group but upon my acceptance of my "true self" and my oneness with the divine. I have finally acknowledged that the past is gone and the future is uncertain. Now is my time to seek out and capture reality. My epiphany has been gradual but worth searching and waiting for.

Early on, no one took the time to analyze my personality and the complex web of uncertainty that I would weave for myself. Those people with whom I associated allowed me to remain behind my psychological bars and often in solitary confinement within the virtual, self-imposed mental institution that restricted me from becoming the person I could have been.

My secrets and psychological discomfort were not awful. They included primarily fears, a lack of confidence and uncertainty. I couldn't accept the portrait that others had of me, yet I couldn't bring myself to change that portrait either. What they thought of me is what I thought I wanted to become and should become. The portrait was usually a fast-moving kaleidoscope of events, impressions and ideas with little permanence. No two psychological pictures were the same, nor did any one picture remain for a period of time.

I never really felt I knew my family. We were always, if not at odds, at different stages of development or levels of understanding. I didn't want to be hurt, even though I was at times; I didn't want to hurt anyone. I couldn't comfortably fight back and, as a result, often remained silent even when I had a strong opinion.

After my marriage, I gradually saw myself changing with the encouragement of my wife. I liked what I saw and felt and determined to become a person confident and joyful within myself.

I enjoyed fifteen minutes of fame prior to and following the Islamic Revolution. I was interviewed by various international reporters in Iran, sought after by diplomats as a possible conduit for negotiating the release of the American hostages and asked to tell my story to conference participants and groups throughout California and on the radio. Perhaps these few minutes in the limelight made me overconfident—for a while after the series of media interviews and in-person presentations I was certain I could accomplish almost anything. After all, I was becoming well known and accepted as a commentator on the Middle East, particularly Iran. My future was promising.

Sadly, none of my dreams materialized. I could not find a job. Most of my contacts had either passed on or retired. I tried hard each day to connect with someone who could offer me work, but toward the end of the day, I would panic, return to our condominium or walk the streets of Santa Rosa, California with Mahin, completely forlorn.

At night, Mahin and I would sit in the living room of the small condominium we had purchased at a twelve percent interest rate with the few funds we had been able to smuggle out of Iran and fret over my lack of success in discovering employment. We could see our small nest egg dwindling every day. What would we do when the few thousand dollars we had were finished? Not her usual positive self, Mahin would inquire each night, "Frank, what appointments do you have tomorrow? Do any of the contacts look promising?" Most often I wouldn't answer. What could I say? I seemed to be hitting my head against a blank wall.

For months, I attempted to avoid any news programs and would surf the television channels for programs that might lift my spirits. Both Mahin and I frequently asked ourselves why we had been put in the position in which we found ourselves. We often wondered why the news media focused on the negative developments in Iran while completely ignoring the plight of families like ours. I believe deep down, we knew the reason but didn't want to admit that controversy and conflict are far more newsworthy than the condition, however impoverished, of one or even numerous families.

Gradually, the level of frustration began to affect both Mahin and me greatly. We would vent to each other but felt we could not let our daughters know what was going on financially or psychologically. After all, they were both young and very impressionable. I slowly realized that celebrity did not guarantee the utopia I had thought it would. I again began to question my personal world and the society to which we had been forced to return. I seemed to have few, if any, choices for the future. Interpersonal honesty seemed illusive. People didn't really seem to care about the plight of Iran or our family. The Islamic Revolution was merely something to talk about and to quiz us about.

Mahin and I discovered that while we were not physically isolated, we were alone in our plight. From my experiences in Iran I had come to believe that people were caring and kind, but the treatment we received after our return to the U.S. following the Islamic Revolution proved that, with few exceptions, we were on our own in a world that seemed cruel and unforgiving. Many people expressed empathy and even sympathy, but few showed any interest in helping or even in finding out how they might be of assistance. A conversation seldom occurred. The extent of the verbal exchange was: "What an unfortunate but interesting experience you have had ... We wish you the best ... You will be all right" The implication was, "Don't bother us." We have our own problems and don't have time to think about your situation."

Clubs and participants in political gatherings loved to hear about our experiences and plight but would leave the scene immediately without engaging in any sort of informal exchange. They seemed to consider our situation the fodder for a novel or short story. We seemed to represent an anomaly that could temporarily serve as a distraction from their daily lives and then be dismissed or forgotten immediately.

I began to withdraw again into my virtual Pepper Tree Kingdom. The persona that had persisted for so many years before my journey to Iran began to re-emerge. My sense of abandonment grew exponentially.

I didn't, however, completely fall apart. Thank God, I had Mahin and our children. I determined to learn from my bad choices and the fate the Revolution had thrust on my family and me. I found living with and loving the family allowed the evolution of a bond that could not be readily broken.

The one thing I did not fully realize until Mahin's death was how precious and short time was and is. I often feel her touch at night when I am in bed alone. And I ask myself why I wasted so much time fretting over petty details and neglecting to tell her more often how much I cared for her.

Following the death, for more than a year I dug into the past and heightened the search for my identity; suddenly one morning I realized that what I had searched for all my life I already possessed and could enjoy with Mahin even in her spirit form. I had a God-given persona of which I could be proud and thankful, a persona that many people could relate to and interact with. Self-change was not necessary. My challenge for the remainder of my life on this earth should be achieving oneness with God and basking in His glory.

What a relief my growing and gradual epiphany has brought to me. I no longer have to pretend to myself or anyone else. I can be myself and know that I belong to "the beloved" and have total freedom through Christ and my submission to His will.

Most of the time throughout the day and night I think to myself, "I'm here, and God is with me." I spend each day laughing, reminiscing and searching for greater truth and depth of spirit. When darkness of spirit attempts to invade my world, I light the sparklers of prayer and watch the fireworks of joy and satisfaction shoot off.

I have come to love silence as much as I enjoy the chatter and conversation of friends and relatives. I can honestly say I have come to enjoy others and life in general.

I have slowly determined to take advantage of each moment and revel in the present rather than regretting the past and fearing the future.

Chapter 24

>>>))((((<<

Finding New Life after Death:
Toward My True Self

The small burial vault, often referred to as a crypt, is located at the far end of the Queen of Heaven cemetery in Lafayette, California. Its marble façade reflects the morning sun and softens the afternoon shadows. It is only one of several final resting places and is dwarfed by the larger crypts under and near the covered area that provides refuge to mourners and visitors. It contains Mahin's ashes and represents a major change in my life.

Beautiful hills frame the cemetery and complement the well-kept grounds. Flowering plants are rare. The deer that inhabit the area tend to devour any live blossoms rather quickly. Artificial flowers are the norm.

The artificial flowers may, at first, depress the visitor. They appear to be without life, only reflecting once breathing and joyful human beings. But further reflection reveals they, like the bodies to which they relate, are long-lasting, require no repotting, have no need for water and can be used to brighten dark corners as can the memories of those who have gone before.

Whether it is the dead of winter or the middle of summer, sadness seems to dissipate when a visitor enters the gate of the cemetery. When a breath of wind blows, a mourner can feel God is whispering to him or her. When the weather is very cold, the mourner's breath hints at the presence of a kindness and gentleness that soothe the wounded soul. When I am near where Mahin rests, I tend to relax in the assurance that she is safe and in good hands.

If I remain at the graveside for an extended period of time, I begin to recall our years together: the days as students; the fun times in Europe and other parts of the world; the births of our two daughters in Iran; the construction of our home in Iran in which I thought we would live for many years; our flight to the United States after the Islamic Revolution; the years we struggled and toiled to make up for our heavy financial losses in Iran; our final days together. I begin talking to myself, waiting for Mahin to answer me. And eventually she does, in a way that reminds me she is still with me.

In her short volume entitled *Heartbroken Open: A Memoir Through Loss to Self-Discovery*, Kristine Carlson declared that even though she understood that grieving could be important to her after the death of her husband, she determined to live in the moment so that she could heal more quickly and continue living life to its fullest. Within two plus years following his death she became ready to "take the wheel" herself. She realized that love was "eternal and formless." Her husband would always be in her heart.

Ms. Carlson's feelings and determination reflect my thoughts or I reflect her feelings and thoughts precisely. Was I ready for Mahin's departure? Absolutely not. The first two years were extremely difficult. From the outset of my journey without my long-time partner, however, I knew I had no choice but to accept the loss and move on. I had to continue my search for and build a strong identity. I purposed to pilot my own ship with God's guidance and make the best of every situation. Mahin remains in my heart, but memories of her do not burden me. They help set me free to live, serve and love with greater intensity.

Mahin's death encouraged me to focus on my future, and the future looks promising. I can picture Christmas dinners with my daughters and grandchildren. I envision travel both near and far. Even though my eyesight may dim, I will be able, with God's help and grace, to share my experiences and insights both orally and in writing. Perhaps, I can even have a say in matters related to international affairs. I will not be shaken but will calmly and deliberately progress in my search for my complete identity without retreating into my virtual Pepper Tree Kingdom.

I returned to the edge of the tall, virtual pepper tree. Its branches hung close to the ground in a semi-weeping fashion, its dense clusters of red berries beckoned to me. The scent of pepper teased my nostrils.

But I refused to allow the virtual tree to envelop me. I didn't need a kingdom in which I was the only inhabitant. I needed and determined to pursue life with zest and in the company of friends and family.

Epilogue

>>>))(((<<

In 2010, four years after Mahin's death, my cousin Helen and I found ourselves in Los Angeles and decided to visit where we'd been born and where Grandma Dickson lived next to the pepper tree that had constituted my imaginary kingdom. I hoped the tree was still there. I didn't want to re-enter my kingdom but did long to know if the tree still existed. After all, the tree had been a significant part of my childhood.

Instead of a tree, we found buildings, most of which appeared to have been constructed a number of years before. Not even a remnant of the tree trunk could be found. Only the small, rundown cottage in which Grandma Dickson had lived remained.

As I stood thinking about the tree and its consoling features, I suddenly envisioned how it had once protected me and saw Mahin's face shining from the imaginary leaves. That invigorating moment prompted me to pen a poem in honor of my roots.

The Healing Pepper Tree

The tree stood alone on an ugly, vacant lot,
unaware of the healing and solace it brought.
Its clusters of pinkish fruit in fall and winter
complemented this ferny-leaf, season-weary ginter.
Almost every day I sat on my rope throne

under its drooping branches,
conducting my imaginary court,
where I took no chances.
I had no crown to wear,
but I was king of a private lair.
I dreamed of ancient history and things international
while I swung like a carefree acrobat,
somewhat irrational.
I never climbed the tree's trunk
but often sat there like an enlightened monk.
My love affair with the pepper tree
lasted what seemed like an eternity.
Long last I left the neighborhood
headed for a destiny not fully understood.
I never really said goodbye to the pepper tree,
thinking I might return to rest once again
in perfect harmony.
Some forty years passed before I made my way back
to the pepper tree under which I had felt no lack.
Alas, my tree was gone,
replaced with buildings to which I was not drawn.
From the buildings I could hear the pepper tree call,
"Where have you been? Why did I have to fall?"
I had no answer, nor could I speak.
My inner emotions made me terribly weak.
I often think of my childhood kingdom,
but quickly realize I would now suffer from boredom
if I lived in the place of the pepper tree.
I can only pretend by using my virtual kingdom key.

Acknowledgments

>>>>)))((((<<<<

Special thanks for the completion of *The Pepper Tree Kingdom* go to my editor, Janice De Jesus and my publisher Karen Mireau. Both Janice and Karen have been extremely patient and tactful; both are highly skilled.

My thanks also to Joshua Sullivan who devoted a great deal of time and energy to the development of the beautiful cover art and to Joe Kauffman, who took the author photograph for this book.

Lastly, I would also like to acknowledge the help of my cousin, Helen Burroughs, who read the manuscript and provided valuable input and support.

About the Author

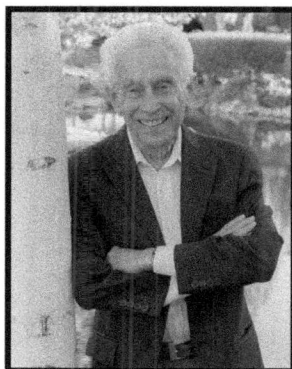

>>>>>))(<<<<<

Franklin T. Burroughs was born in Wilmington, California and attended elementary school in Arkansas, completing his formal education in California.

After obtaining his Doctorate of Education degree in Middle East Studies and Comparative Education from the University of California, Los Angeles, he did post-doctoral work in Islamic Studies at the University of Tehran. He later lived and worked in both Iran and Saudi Arabia.

A writer, university professor and businessman, Frank has published numerous articles and essays. He currently lives in northern California near his two daughters and their families, where he is working on his next book.

The author welcomes your comments
and communication.
You can reach him directly at:
ftburroughs@att.net

Azalea Art Press
specializes in giving personal attention
to authors who wish to realize
their literary and creative dreams.

AZALEA

ART PRESS

To learn more about writing,
designing and successfully marketing
your next print, e-reader or e-book,
please get in touch with:

Karen Mireau
Azalea.Art.Press@gmail.com
azaleaartpress.blogspot.com

510.919.6117

To schedule an interview or signing
with the author, please contact the publisher.
This memoir by Franklin T. Burroughs
may be ordered directly at
www.lulu.com.

www.ingramcontent.com/pod-product-compliance
Lightning Source LLC
Chambersburg PA
CBHW021049090426
42738CB00006B/255